THE
LUMBER BOOM
OF COASTAL SOUTH CAROLINA

THE
LUMBER BOOM
OF COASTAL SOUTH CAROLINA

*Nineteenth-Century Shipbuilding &
the Devastation of Lowcountry Virgin Forests*

Robert McAlister

Charleston   London

THE
History
PRESS

Published by The History Press
Charleston, SC 29403
www.historypress.net

First published 2013

Manufactured in the United States

ISBN 978.1.62619.278.2

Library of Congress CIP data applied for.

Contents

Foreword, by Harriott Hampton Faucette   7
Acknowledgements   9
Introduction   11

1. 1825–35: Henry Buck of Bucksport, Maine, Establishes the First
   Steam Sawmill in South Carolina   13
2. 1835–60: Buck's Mills Become the Largest Supplier of South
   Carolina Lumber to the Shipbuilders of Maine   23
3. 1860–75: The Buck Family Survives the Civil War and Resumes
   Lumber Shipments to the North   31
4. The Legacy of the *Henrietta* and Northeastern Shipbuilding   39
5. 1885–1900: The Decline of Bucksville and the Buck Family's
   Lumber Mills   59
6. 1900–30: The Atlantic Coast Lumber Corporation, the Largest
   Lumber Mill East of the Mississippi River   67
7. International Paper Company in Georgetown, the Largest Single
   Paper Mill in the World   81
8. Forest Restoration and Conservation in Lowcountry South Carolina   85

Epilogue: Summer in the Swamps   97
Bibliography   107
Index   109
About the Author   111

Foreword

As the daughter of the late Harry Hampton, who has often been called the "father of conservation" in South Carolina, I found Mac McAlister's well-researched history about the forests and waterways of the Lowcountry to be a fascinating education.

While I'm quite familiar with the woods and waters near the center of the state, I know nothing about these matters in the Lowcountry. While South Carolinians take pride in being descended from the owners of great rice plantations, Mac points out how much forest was destroyed to clear the way for rice fields. The beautiful woodlands are gone, as are the great rice plantations—another example of man's shortsightedness in placing too little value on the natural environment.

For many years—in fact, decades—my father contacted politicians, nationally known biologists, botanists, arborists and ornithologists in an effort to gain support for his fight to save the last of the old-growth bottomland forests from being cut for timber. He traveled all over the state, speaking to groups he thought might be interested. He even endured booing and insults from people who opposed him.

John Cely, noted conservationist and author of *Cowasee Basin*, recalls meeting my father when John was an undergraduate at Clemson. My father took him to the Congaree to see some of the champion trees. During their time together, he thought, "Here's a man fifty years older than I am who thinks just like me." Apparently, "Crazy Old Harry," as some called him, was simply ahead of his time!

This bottomland cypress forest in Congaree National Park shows how Lowcountry swamps looked before logging began. *Photo by Mary McAlister.*

In the 1970s, when my father was of advanced age and suffering health issues, a group of like-minded young people rallied to the cause. Their activist cry was, "Congaree Action Now!" Thanks to their youth, passion and energy, they succeeded in winning public and political support. In 1976, Congress declared the area to be Congaree National Monument.

Although my father died four years later, he had lived to see the place he treasured protected forever. He never dreamed that it would later become the Congaree National Park, complete with the Harry Hampton Visitors Center.

Having been lost alone in the Congaree for some twenty-two hours in 2003, I have acquired the nickname "Swamp Woman," a moniker Mac McAlister is fond of using.

—**Harriott Hampton Faucette**

Acknowledgements

I have received invaluable help in writing this book from many sources. Mrs. Pat Adams of Bucksville, Maine, furnished genealogical records of the Buck and McGilvery families and historical information about her town. Cipperly Good and the staff of the Penobscot Marine Museum in Searsport, Maine, provided images and much information about the ship *Henrietta*. Monica Pattangall, family historian of Lenox, Massachusetts, provided information about the Nickels family and about vessels that traveled to and from Bucksville, South Carolina. The *Independent Republic Quarterly* reports, published by the Horry County Historical Society, were a valuable resource concerning the Buck family. Thanks to those members and acquaintances of the Buck family who contributed articles to the *IRQ*, including Charles Joyner, Eugenia Buck Cutts, Constance Fournier, Charles Dusenbury, William H. Pendleton and Sharyn Holliday. Mrs. Henry L. Buck IV of Upper Mill gave me valuable information and allowed access to the original Henry Buck home. Mr. Sidney Thompson was helpful and gave access to Hebron Methodist Church. Mrs. Mary Owens provided much information about the African American community of Bucksport, South Carolina. Julie Warren of the Georgetown County Digital Library provided scans of images of the Atlantic Coast Lumber Corporation and other subjects. Mr. Michael Prevost provided information about forest conservation efforts in South Carolina. Members of the South Carolina Forestry Commission were helpful with historic images and information. Cheryl Oakes of the Forest History Society of Duke University provided a copy of the 1916 article in *American Lumberman* about the Atlantic Coast Lumber Corporation. Christine Ellis of the Winyah River Foundation provided information about river conservation. Ben Burroughs of the Horry County Archives Center at Coastal Carolina University provided images and information about the Buck family.

Thanks to John Sands, director of the Lowcountry Program for the Gaylord and Dorothy Donnelley Foundation, for reviewing the manuscript. I also thank Phillip Wilkinson for his help during our IP canal adventure of 1954. Many thanks to Harriott Hampton Faucette for the foreword and to Cecelia Dailey for reviewing the text and images. Thanks to The History Press for editing the manuscript. My wife, Mary, gave invaluable help by taking photographs and providing ideas and patience during the process.

Introduction

Hundreds of years ago, forests of longleaf pine, bald cypress and oak covered much of the Lowcountry of South Carolina. As far back as colonial times, the tall pines, sturdy live oaks and rot-resistant cypress trees were valued for shipbuilding, both here and in New England and England. After the Buck family relocated from Maine to the banks of the Waccamaw River in the 1820s, the shipbuilders of Maine and the sawmills of South Carolina developed a lasting relationship. The largest wooden sailing ship ever built in South Carolina was built in 1875 in Bucksville, South Carolina, upriver from Georgetown.

It was the lumber barons of the Northeast and Midwest who succeeded in destroying the old-growth forests of South Carolina during the early twentieth century after having been used for generations by smaller industries. A visit to Congaree National Park, which contains the largest stand of bottomland hardwoods in the southeastern United States, will show anyone the various species and sizes of magnificent trees in the Lowcountry before the lumber boom. Located outside of Columbia, South Carolina, the inland Congaree forest is about one hundred miles from coastal Georgetown. It was only after 90 percent of old-growth forests were gone that forestry conservationists began the long, slow process of reforesting.

What follows is the story of Henry Buck and his settlement near Georgetown, the rise and decline of the lumber and shipbuilding industries, the forests in the context of rice production, the modern-day paper industry and conservation efforts in this region. Buck was a venture capitalist, building a business within the laws of his times. His reality was one that included slave labor, and the timber industry was thriving nationwide. With so much of our old-growth forests gone today, it is important to see how they were exploited to understand the value and commodities that a restored forest supplies. Presented here is a greater tale of how an industry can boom and bust, stripping the land of what should be a renewable resource.

Chapter 1

1825–35

Henry Buck of Bucksport, Maine, Establishes the First Steam Sawmill in South Carolina

While passing through the "pine barrens" of South Carolina in the nineteenth century, Englishman Charles Mackay wrote:

Where, northward as you go,
The pines forever grow;
Where, southward if you bend,
Are pine-trees without end;
Where, if you travel west,
Earth loves the pine-tree best;
Where, eastward if you gaze,
Through long, unvaried ways;
Behind you and before
Are pine-trees evermore.

On any clear, sunny day in 1820, someone might look down from the sky at the flat Atlantic coast of South Carolina and see miles of white sandy beaches along its barrier islands and mainland shore, interrupted by brown, winding rivers emptying into deltas at their mouths. Lowland swamps on either side of the rivers and in between are green with the crowns of virgin bald cypress, oaks and vast forests of tall loblolly and longleaf pines, stretching west toward sand hills one hundred miles away. Charleston is the only settlement recognized as a city, positioned on a peninsula at the mouths of two rivers. Fifty miles north of Charleston is

Aerial photograph of abandoned rice fields along the Waccamaw River. *Courtesy of David Soliday.*

another indentation in the coastline that joins four rivers and empties into the Atlantic Ocean. At the upper end of Winyah Bay is a small settlement, Georgetown, and above that town, along the banks of the rivers, are hundreds of squares of cultivated lowland, each separated from the river by earthen dikes. Inside of each small square grows the crop that makes its owners the wealthiest men in America: rice.

The rice planters along the Waccamaw, Pee Dee, Black and Santee Rivers of South Carolina were descendants of English and French Huguenot settlers who had come to America long before the Revolution. By 1825, they were part of a third generation of rice planters, who produced half of all rice grown in America. Profits from the sale of rice were immense. Owners of rice plantations were the equivalent of the English aristocracy, living in palatial white-columned mansions scattered along the shores of the rivers. They and their families entertained each other with lavish dinners, and many met at the Hot and Hot Fish Club along the Waccamaw River to drink claret or whiskey and swap stories about hunting, fishing and politics. Although the plantations were separated from Charleston's more civilized society by over fifty miles of swamps and thick forests, the planters often traveled by boat to that city, where they owned town houses in fashionable parts of

1802 Drayton map of the rivers of South Carolina. *Taken from* A View of South Carolina, *by Governor John Drayton.*

Charleston and enjoyed the balls of the St. Cecelia Society and horse races at the Jockey Club. In summer, when hot and humid air hung over their rice fields, they escaped to other homes on beaches or in the mountains, leaving their white overseers to manage the labor of thousands of black slaves, who were the reason that the luxurious lifestyle of the gentry was possible.[1]

---

1. Because there are so many gaps in the historical record about the lives of the characters presented here, I often imagine how one might have seen and interacted with the environment. Putting myself in the shoes of Henry Buck, for example, the narrative of his discovery of the forests and shipbuilding resources is illuminated according to my research.

During the spring of 1825, one of the wealthiest South Carolina rice planters, a colonel by the name of Allston, was returning from Charleston to his plantation along the Waccamaw River aboard a steamboat. As the boat neared Georgetown, Colonel Allston was standing on deck in the early morning observing the tall, white, almost-new lighthouse at the entrance to Winyah Bay when a poorly dressed stranger approached him and introduced himself as Henry Buck from Bucksport, Maine. Colonel Allston was not particularly interested in conversing with a common Yankee, but he listened to Henry Buck as he explained why he was there and what he wanted. Allston concluded that the only thing they had in common was their age: twenty-five.

Henry told Colonel Allston that Bucksport, Maine, was a small coastal town along the Penobscot River, where most men were sailors, boat builders or fishermen. Henry Buck was the great-grandson of the founder of Bucksport, Jonathan Buck. Henry's father, Ebenezer, was a carpenter, not a wealthy man. Henry had worked in the shipyards of Searsport and Bucksport since he was a boy. However, Henry wasn't satisfied to stay in Maine for the rest of his life. A year ago, while he was working in a Searsport shipyard, a Charleston-built ship had laid up there for repairs. While she was on the ways, he had admired the dense live oak—almost as hard as iron—of the ship's knees. He had run his hands along the ship's pine planking, which was harder than the white pine from Maine's forests. He had been impressed by the beautiful clear cypress paneling in the aft cabin. All of these timbers, he had been told, were cut from vast forests in South Carolina. He knew that the pitch and tar he used on the seams and rigging of ships had come from pine trees in South Carolina. He wanted to see for himself where these trees grew, so he had shipped out for Charleston aboard a New England sailing vessel. In Charleston, he had been told that the best timberland was located along rivers north of Georgetown. He asked the distinguished Colonel Allston where he might find such land available for purchase. Allston replied that all lands north of Georgetown were in use as rice plantations and that none of the planters would ever sell. Colonel Allston's only suggestion was that Buck book passage on a small steamer that made weekly trips up the Waccamaw River toward the village of Conwayborough. Conwayborough, he said, was too far upstream for the growing of rice, and cheaper land might be found near there.

The steamboat tied up alongside a wharf in Georgetown, no longer a bustling city. During the early 1700s, Georgetown had been a shipbuilding town, using live oak, cypress and pine to build sizeable vessels. By 1800, shipbuilding had moved to New England, and Georgetown was left with a few run-down stores bordering its main street along the Sampit River. Henry Buck found a rustic rooming house, where he spent the night. The next day, he was able to find a boat to take him up the Waccamaw River thirty miles toward Conwayborough. During the first part of the trip, Buck looked past the tall grass of salt marshes on both sides of the wide river at magnificent bald cypress trees with feathery green needles and gray trunks as thick as five or six feet, some towering one hundred feet above the river. In the distance, behind the marshes and cypress swamps, was a wall of tall pines. As the boat traveled farther upstream, he saw the earthen dikes that protected rice fields from the rise of river water at high tide. Rice fields stretched for miles along both sides of the river. He saw black slaves working in some of the fields. Farther up the river, there were no rice fields. Cypress swamps and pine-covered bluffs bordered the narrow winding river until they reached a landing a few miles below Conwayborough. Buck had never seen trees as thick and tall as these in his entire life. From the landing, he rode in a buggy along a rough, shaded path through a thick, dark forest to Conwayborough. Conwayborough was the principal town in the Horry District of South Carolina and was named after Revolutionary War general Peter Horry, who had fought under General Francis Marion.

Henry Buck knew he had come to the right place. He looked up at the magnificent pine trees and thought of ship's planking and decking that each tree would make when cut down, sawn into lumber and delivered to a shipyard in Maine. Deciding to remain in Conwayborough, Henry Buck lived at a rooming house run by Mrs. Sarah Jane Norman. While looking for suitable timberland, he found an opportunity to run a store at Grissetts Landing, three miles above Conwayborough. He took over the Grissetts Landing store and, a few months later, was able to find and buy a few hundred acres of inexpensive virgin timberland bordering the Waccamaw River a few miles below Conwayborough. On that land grew hundreds of tall pine, oak and cypress trees, which Buck hoped to harvest and send back to Maine.

Buck noticed that farmers who owned high land near his had slashed the bark of hundreds of longleaf pines to make turpentine from the sap. Most of the trees had rectangular boxes cut into their bases to catch sap that ran down from a series of deep gouges that had been cut higher up on the face of the tree. During the spring and summer months, they and their slaves dipped out the sap that ran down from the gouges in the trunk and into the boxes. They ladled the sap into barrels and carted them to a copper still.

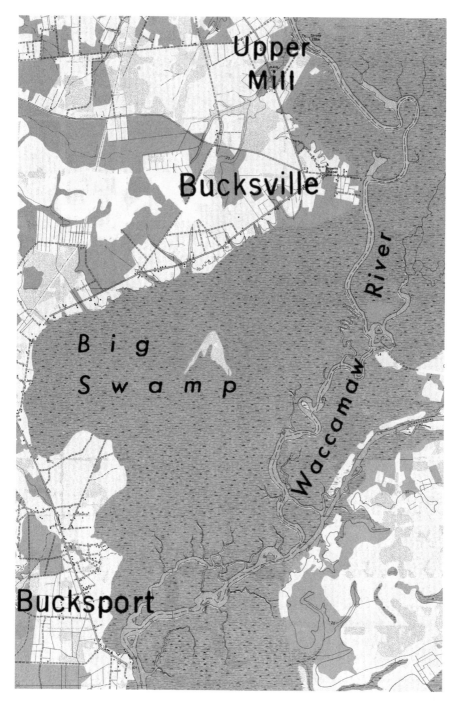

Henry Buck's properties along the Waccamaw River. Conwayborough is to the north. Tip Top, Sandy Island and Georgetown are to the south. *Courtesy of Cecelia Dailey.*

A 160-foot-tall loblolly pine in Congaree National Park. There were other such pines in Lowcountry forests before the lumber boom. *Photo by Mary McAlister.*

The sap, or resin, was boiled in the still, which separated it into turpentine and rosin. Turpentine and rosin were then poured into wooden barrels for shipment. Not far from the turpentine shed was a pit in the ground, where resinous pine branches were covered and smoldered slowly, releasing liquid tar, which ran to the lowest point in the pit. The tar was ladled into barrels for shipment. Some of the tar was boiled to make pitch. He watched barrels of naval stores, turpentine tar and pitch, being loaded onto flats to be poled down the river to Georgetown, where they would be sold to merchants and transported by ship to Charleston and cities in the Northeast. Buck also

Above: An old-growth longleaf pine forest ready to be logged. *Courtesy of South Carolina Forestry Commission.*

Left: A barefoot man prepares to float a raft of giant logs down the river to a sawmill. *Courtesy of Georgetown County Digital Library.*

noticed that many of the gouged trees were dead. No young trees were taking their place, mainly because pine seedlings were being rooted up or eaten by hogs that farmers allowed to roam free through the forests. Farmers told Buck that they and their fathers before them had been relying on the sale of "dip" since way before the American Revolution. They saw an inexhaustible supply of pine trees and planned to continue selling naval stores as long as people would buy them. Buck noticed that other farmers had cut down or set fire to tracts of pine trees that were in their way so that they could clear fields to graze cattle or plant cotton.

Henry Buck walked through his forest, listening to the quietness of the wind through the pines. He was astonished by the size and height of

A turpentiner ladles "dip" into a bucket from a boxed longleaf pine. *Courtesy of South Carolina Forestry Commission.*

A tar pit loaded with resinous branches ready to be burned for tar and pitch. *Courtesy of South Carolina Forestry Commission.*

many of the pines on his high land. Long needles and big cones covered the ground around them. Some of the bark of the trees was scorched, as fires had burned away brush but had not killed the young pines. Nearer the riverbank were a few widely spaced live oak trees, gnarled and magnificent, stretching their giant limbs far out in all directions. He knew that as long ago as colonial times, the natural crooks of their curved limbs had been valued for toughness and strength in building ships' framing. In the swamps along the bank of the river were the huge bald cypress trees. He had been told that some might be one thousand years old. During the first months, Buck grew to love his land in South Carolina. On his walks through the woods, he saw deer, otters, alligators, raccoons, possums and other creatures. He had been told there were bears, but he hadn't seen any. He had heard the screech of bobcats, the howls of wolves, the loud hammer of woodpeckers and the calls of owls and other birds that he didn't recognize. He shot a wild turkey and took it back to the boardinghouse to be cooked for dinner. In April, spring-green needles and leaves sprouted in the forest while snow still covered the ground back in Maine. The blues and yellows of wildflowers and the smell of jasmine and honeysuckle were everywhere along the river.

Chapter 2
1835–60

Buck's Mills Become the Largest Supplier of South Carolina Lumber to the Shipbuilders of Maine

Although Henry Buck wanted to build a sawmill on his land right away, he knew he must find financial backing and a market for his lumber. He returned to Bucksport, Maine, and started work in a shipyard while he looked for financial help from relatives and friends for his venture in South Carolina. While in Searsport, Maine, he met an attractive lady, Mary Clark from Gouldsboro. They fell in love and were married in 1827. Not long afterward, Henry Buck made an arrangement with a ship owner in Searsport, who agreed to lend him money to finance a sawmill in South

Henry Buck (1800–1870). *Courtesy of Mrs. Henry L. Buck IV.*

Carolina and to send a ship to pick up the lumber when it was ready. Buck wanted to get started immediately. Henry and Mary agreed that she would stay behind, as there was no suitable home for them in the woods where he was going.

Buck returned to his land alone. He needed help with the labor of cutting trees and sawing lumber. He knew that his only source of labor would be slaves. He visited an Allston rice planter who owned a plantation several miles downstream from his property and who was a relative of the Allston that he had met on his first trip to South Carolina. Because the rice-harvest season was over, this Colonel Allston agreed to rent a few field hands to Henry Buck. With their help, Henry built a log cabin for himself and began to cut down longleaf pine trees with axes and saws. During those early days of exploring and clearing his land along the river, he might have discovered the remains of an ancient Indian cypress dugout canoe, half buried in the mud. He probably would have wondered how long ago the canoe had been burned and hacked out without metal tools and what kind of people lived in these swamps so long ago. He knew that before the English arrived, this part of Lowcountry South Carolina had been populated for thousands of years by tribes of Indians who had hunted, fished and lived in the forests without destroying them. The grandfather of one of Henry's slaves might have been an Indian at a time when Indians and blacks were both being enslaved by the English.

After Henry and a slave had notched and felled the first pine tree, he counted its annual rings, so closely spaced that he lost count after 150. With axes and adzes, they squared the trunk into a rough heart-pine beam and sawed it into lengths. Resin oozed from the saw cuts. The beam was so heavy that they couldn't lift it and had to cut it into shorter lengths so that a team of oxen could drag the beams to the riverbank. Henry worked alongside his slaves to cut down and square up more trees, drag them to the riverbank and stack them. Buck had slaves dig a deep pit for the sawing of some beams into boards. To split a squared beam with a pit saw, one man stood in the bottom of the pit and another on a stand over the pit, slowly sawing the beam from one end to the other. It took over a month of steady hard work to cut enough lumber to fill a small vessel. Buck had given word to the Maine ship owner as to when the lumber would be ready. When the Maine schooner arrived in Georgetown, it was towed up the Waccamaw River to a landing that Buck had prepared. When the loading of the schooner was complete, Buck sent the slaves back to their owner. Henry Buck was aboard the loaded schooner, which drew over ten feet of water, as it was towed twenty miles down the shallow Waccamaw River to Georgetown and was anchored to await the next favorable tide. A harbor pilot was aboard the schooner as it sailed ten miles along Winyah Bay's narrow channel and across the bar into the Atlantic Ocean. With a favorable wind, it took over a week to clear Cape Hatteras and reach its destination of Searsport along the Penobscot River. When the shipyard owner saw the beautiful heart-pine timbers, he was pleased and paid Henry a high price for them.

Mary Buck greeted Henry with a newborn son, William Lightfoot, born in February 1828 while Henry was in South Carolina. Henry now had enough money to buy more land and machinery for a steam-powered sawmill, but he still had no house for his family. He returned alone to South Carolina with sawmill machinery aboard the ship. He bought more land

and slaves and began his sawmill operation, which was the first steam-powered sawmill in South Carolina. Slaves cut down pine trees, dragged them with ox carts to a bank of the river, bundled the logs into long rafts and floated them with the tide to the sawmill. At first, Henry made beams and boards from only the heartwood of trees, discarding the rest. Later, he learned that all of the wood from longleaf pine trees was marketable. He built a landing and wharf for ships to load lumber. He kept in touch with shipbuilders in Bucksport, Searsport and Bath, who sent ships to load his lumber. He also tapped some longleaf pines for naval stores, bought a

The chimney for Henry Buck's 1828 sawmill, Upper Mill, along the Waccamaw River. *Courtesy of Mrs. Henry L. Buck IV.*

Henry Buck's home at Upper Mill, built in 1828. *Courtesy of Mrs. Henry L. Buck IV.*

turpentine still and had barrels made to ship pitch and turpentine. He built a house along the Waccamaw River next to the sawmill and named the Rothmahler Bluff property Upper Mill Plantation.

Henry Buck returned regularly to Maine, and in 1830, a daughter, Mary Jane, was born. Henry's wife, Mary, told him that she had no desire to leave her home in Maine to live in South Carolina. Henry gave her an ultimatum: unless she returned with him to South Carolina, he would divorce her and take the two children with him. She refused, and they were divorced. Henry Buck took William and Mary Jane Buck to his house at Upper Mill. Mary Clark Buck eventually remarried in Maine.

Buck's lumber business increased, and his sawmill became one of the largest in the area. He bought the rights to cut trees on properties of other nearby landowners, and he bought trees that other landowners cut and floated down to his mill. He was able to process more lumber than the Maine shipyards in Bucksport and Searsport wanted to buy. Henry sought to find additional markets for his lumber through the help of his wealthy Bucksport cousin, Richard Pike Buck, who had opened a transportation and shipping business in New York City in 1828. He helped Henry Buck obtain orders to sell pine and oak lumber in the West Indies, South America and Europe.

Henry Buck stayed in contact with the Norman family in Conwayborough, where he had first lived. He couldn't have helped but notice that Sarah Jane

Norman's daughter, Frances, had grown into an attractive young woman. She was twenty years old at that time, and Henry soon fell in love with her. He married Frances Norman in 1838, and they and his children lived in his home at Upper Mill.

In 1837, Henry Buck and a partner purchased 432 acres at Murdock's Landing, several miles south of Upper Mill, and built another steam sawmill. He named this property Lower Mill, which later became Bucksport. Between Upper Mill and Lower Mill, at Hillens Landing, a competitor, John Pickett, bought land and built a steam sawmill in 1838. Pickett operated his sawmill at Hillens Landing only until 1841, when Henry Buck expanded his business by buying Pickett's property and sawmill. He called this property Middle Mill, which later became Bucksville. He replaced the existing mill with a thirty-horsepower steam sawmill, the largest in the Georgetown-Horry area. He built wharves for a quarter mile along the Waccamaw River, where several ships could be loaded at one time. The Bucksville community surrounding the sawmill grew until it was as large or larger than Conwayborough.

Henry Buck expanded his slave labor force, which numbered more than one hundred men and women by 1850 and more than three hundred in 1860. He treated his slaves better than some of the rice plantation owners. James Gilmore, a journalist from the North who visited Henry Buck in December 1860 and who later wrote *Among the Pines* about his visit, stated:

> *His "family" of slaves numbered about three hundred, and were a more healthy, and to all appearances, happy set of laboring people, I had never seen. Well fed, comfortably and almost neatly clad, with tidy and well-ordered homes, exempt from labor in childhood and advanced age, and cared for in sickness by a kind and considerate mistress, who is the physician and good Samaritan of the village, they seemed to share as much physical enjoyment as ordinarily falls to the lot of the "hewer of wood and drawer of water."*

Buck knew that the toil of cutting and transporting trees to the sawmill was backbreaking work, so he trained some of his older slaves to do the skilled work of running and maintaining the sawmill equipment.

Henry and Frances Buck had seven children between 1838 and 1854. In 1838, Henry's eldest son, William, was ten years old. There was no school or teacher anywhere nearby. Henry didn't want to send him to the Winyah Indigo Society School in Georgetown or to a boarding school in Charleston, so William was sent back to Maine, where he stayed with relatives and was educated in Gorham. As their other children grew to school age, Henry and Frances employed a teacher from Maine. In 1849, Mary Brookman, a cousin of Henry Buck, came south to tutor the Buck children. She married a man from Conwayborough and lived near Bucksville for the rest of her life. She was among several Maine women who married, moved to the Bucksville area and stayed.

During a two-year period at the end of the 1830s, fifty-two lumber-loaded vessels sailed from Bucksville. During the 1840s, Henry Buck's three sawmills worked full time, and the number of ships increased accordingly. Georgetown's port had been stagnant for several years, and most of the ship traffic passing through the port of Georgetown was headed for Bucksville. Most of the rice planters along the rivers sent their rice directly to Charleston for milling and delivery to northeastern and foreign ports. Henry Buck and others petitioned Congress to make Bucksville a port of entry, a request that was opposed by most of Georgetown's citizens and politicians. Henry's request was denied, and Georgetown remained the only port of entry. In November 1845, the *Winyah Observer* listed eleven vessels—nine brigs, one schooner and one sloop—at Bucksville, loading lumber and naval stores for northern and West Indian ports. Many of the vessels entering Bucksville arrived with stone ballast in their holds, which they dumped into the river before they loaded lumber. Round stones from all over New England were soon scattered along the banks of the Waccamaw River. In January 1848, it was reported that twenty-eight vessels loaded lumber at Bucksville. An 1840s Charleston newspaper stated, "Although we are southern born—southern all over—it would be gratifying to see a considerable mixture of Yankee energy and enterprise infused in our people of the genial South." Men who dealt with Henry Buck admitted that he demonstrated what could be accomplished with "Yankee energy." As a result of Buck's success with his lumber mills, he "had amassed a princely fortune." He continued to travel regularly to Maine to visit his son, William, and to meet with business associates in Bucksport and Searsport. He had many friends in Searsport, including a wealthy ship captain and shipyard owner, William McGilvery. Henry Buck supplied McGilvery with pine, cypress and oak for building several vessels. Some of McGilvery's shipyard carpenters moved to Bucksville to work at Buck's sawmill.

In 1848, Henry Buck and others in the Bucksville community decided to build a new Methodist church to replace an earlier one. Many of the materials to build and furnish Hebron Methodist Church were donated by Maine shipbuilders and brought to Bucksville on ships from New England.

Hebron Methodist Church was built in Bucksville, South Carolina, in 1848 by Maine shipwrights. *Photo by Mary McAlister.*

Bricks and stones for the foundation were hauled in as ballast. William McGilvery gave the doors, windows, blinds and a mahogany pulpit for the church. On the day that the structure of the church was to be raised, Henry Buck closed his mill so that his carpenters and laborers could work at the church. Finishing work on the church was done under the supervision of ship's carpenters from Maine. The church had doors at the front for white parishioners and at the rear for slaves to attend services. The Buck family paid most of the expenses to build the church. Henry Buck also set aside land for a Buck family cemetery across from the new church.

In 1841, a member of the Allston family, twenty-year-old J. Motte Alston,[2] gained title to six hundred acres of swampland at the intersection of Bull Creek and the Waccamaw River, just south of Henry Buck's Lower Mill property. J. Motte Alston had grown up as privileged and pampered as the other Allston gentry. The Allstons had owned their several plantations since before the American Revolution and were in their third generation as plantation owners. J. Motte Alston was not in line to inherit any of the existing Allston plantations, so in 1844, he decided to create a new rice plantation on his six hundred acres of swampland, "which had never been touched by an

2. The Allstons and Alstons were different branches of the same family.

axe." Alston stated in his autobiography, *Rice Planter and Sportsman*, "The growth consisted of enormous cypress, gum, ash, etc., matted together with huge grape vines and cane from fifteen to twenty feet high."

Alston hired an overseer and brought eighty slaves to the property to begin the tremendous task of clearing and building dikes for 450 acres of rice fields. Like so many other planters, he destroyed all of the virgin forest that covered the land where he wanted to grow rice. It took several years of backbreaking work to cut and burn the trees, remove the stumps, build high dikes of mud along the river, cut canals and trenches and prepare the fields for planting. J. Motte had been able to borrow money from his family to finance the new rice plantation, which he named Woodbourne. He planted his first crop on 75 acres in 1847, but the crop was washed away by a freshet because the main dike wasn't high enough to hold back the flood. Subsequently, he completed the dikes and had several years of successful crops, making a considerable fortune. He had married a girl from a prominent Georgia planter family and in 1848 moved with her into a new twelve-room house on the Woodbourne property, built for him by a talented slave carpenter. Apparently, there was little or no social contact between J. Motte Alston and Henry Buck, although Alston's overseer occasionally purchased lumber from Buck.

Chapter 3

1860–75

The Buck Family Survives the Civil War and Resumes Lumber Shipments to the North

By 1850, southern yellow "hard pine" was the preferred wood for the planking and decking of almost all ships built in Maine. The flexible fibers and durable surface of longleaf pine boards made them ideal for the hard wear that wooden hulls were subjected to in ocean swells. During the 1850s, Buck's mills were producing three million feet of lumber per year. Henry Buck began to buy shares in vessels built in Maine's shipyards, vessels that he used to haul lumber from his mills. The brig[3] *Lillian* was built in 1851 in Bucksport, Maine, owned jointly by Henry Buck, Richard Pike Buck of New York City and Charles Buck of Boston. Henry Buck took part ownership in other vessels built by William McGilvery in Searsport. In 1852, the bark[4] *Henry Buck*, 149 feet long and 594 tons, was built by William McGilvery in Searsport. When she was overhauled in a Searsport yard in 1870, it was found that "the hard pine timber is perfectly sound, whilst a large portion of the eastern white oak had to be replaced." In 1853, the bark *Fanny Buck*, named for Henry Buck's wife, Frances, was built in Searsport. She was owned by John McGilvery, William McGilvery's brother and shipyard partner. The *Fanny Buck*, 140 feet long and 583 tons, went aground on her maiden voyage

---

3. A brig is a two-masted sailing vessel with the foremast square-rigged and the aft mast rigged fore and aft. Square-rigged masts had horizontal spars, called yardarms, which spread the sails. Fore-and-aft sails were triangular and had no yardarms.
4. A bark is a sailing vessel with three or more masts. The forward masts are square-rigged. The aft mast is rigged fore and aft.

from Searsport and was sold to Norwegians, who renamed her *Martha*. In 1854, the vessel *Winyah* was built in Bucksport, Maine, partially owned by Henry Buck. In 1855, the brig *Waccamaw* was built by William McGilvery in Searsport for Henry Buck. The *Waccamaw*, registered in Bucksville, sailed between Maine and South Carolina for over ten years.

Henry Buck's ship traffic up and down the Waccamaw River grew and grew. J. Motte Alston reported from Woodbourne, "Two miles above Woodbourne on the Waccamaw were large sawmills from which were exported pine lumber of all kinds to the West Indies. These vessels would pass in front of my house, and I would frequently lay in all the fruit I wanted at a trifling cost."

Sometimes, Buck's *Waccamaw* was crewed entirely by slaves, and on one occasion, it was observed by an Allston rice mill overseer, who said, "There is no white man in her when she comes to the mill." In 1859, Captain Edward Clifford of the schooner *James Crosby* wrote to his wife from Charleston, "I want to settle my outward freight and see if Captain McGilvery would want me to go to Bucksville. If he don't, I shall go to another house to see what I can find." Later, he wrote, "I am going to Bucksville—please write to me at that place as soon as you get this."

One vessel loading lumber at Buck's mill was not so lucky. The brig *Joann* loaded lumber at Bucksville and headed for Maine. She was becalmed at the Winyah Bay entrance as she attempted to cross the bar. She anchored but lost her anchor, drifted ashore and filled with water. Her sails and rigging were salvaged, brought to Georgetown and sold at auction.

J. Motte Alston and his wife moved into their new house at Woodbourne in 1849. His rice-planting venture was successful, but it was a lonely existence for Mary Alston, being separated from the plantation social life of the Waccamaw Neck by swamps, Bull Creek and the Waccamaw River. Mary wasn't happy there, even though J. Motte built a summer home for her in Murrells Inlet. She had six children at Woodbourne between 1849 and 1858, at which point J. Motte gave up rice planting, rented out his slaves, sold Woodbourne to Henry Buck and moved with his wife and his fortune to Columbia, South Carolina. Contemplating the sale of Woodbourne, J. Motte Alston said, "I was both pleased and distressed—pleased that I had it in my power to reward my dear Mary for the long years of patient endurance, and grieved at seeing the home of our early married life pass into the hands of strangers."

Only three years later, the age of the rice-planting aristocracy would be ended by the Civil War. Henry Buck used the house at Woodbourne as a summer home for many years, but he changed the name of the plantation to Tip Top.

The Buck family continued to intertwine with Maine shipbuilding families. In 1858, Henry Buck's daughter Lucinda married Cephas Gilbert from Maine, who had moved to South Carolina to manage Buck's Lower Mill at Bucksport. In 1860, Henry Buck's eldest son, William, married Desiah Hichborn McGilvery, daughter of William McGilvery, in Searsport, Maine. William had been looking out for the interests of Henry Buck's lumber business in Maine. Desiah McGilvery had once been engaged to a Searsport ship captain by the name of Amos Nickels, who died at sea before they could be married. It was remarked before her marriage to William Buck that "she lost a Nickel but gained a Buck." Over the course of several generations, a number of members of the Buck, McGilvery and Nickels families intermarried.

By 1860, there were several Maine men and couples living in Bucksville, South Carolina, and as the dispute over secession and arguments over the approaching presidential election grew intense, they were split over whether they favored Unionism or secession. Most of the non–slave owning and relatively poor farmers of South Carolina, who composed 90 percent of the population, were not in favor of secession. Only 3 percent of the population owned slaves. The rice-planter secessionists, including the ones from Georgetown, who owned eighteen thousand slaves, held political power in Charleston. Many of the secessionists believed that the federal government wouldn't dare interfere with the rights of states in the South to secede and form their own slave-owning country. Although Henry Buck was the largest slaveholder in the Horry District, he was strongly against secession. He guessed that the North would not allow the Union to be dissolved and that the South would have to fight a war against a power that was too strong to defeat.

After the election of Abraham Lincoln in November 1860, South Carolina voted overwhelmingly to secede from the Union. Soon after South Carolina seceded, but before the first shots of the Civil War were fired, Henry Buck received a visit from James Gilmore, who was on his way from Charleston to Wilmington, North Carolina. As described in his book *Among the Pines*, he had traveled from Charleston to Georgetown in

> *the little steamer* Nina [a cross between a full-grown nautilus and a half-grown tub], *which a few weeks later was enrolled as the first man-of-war of the Confederate navy. As the embryo war-steamer rounded up to the long, low, rickety dock, lumbered breast-high with cotton, turpentine, and rosin, not a white face was to be seen.*

Gilmore's opinion of Georgetown was not positive:

> *Though situated on a magnificent bay, a little below the confluence of three noble rivers, which drain a country of surpassing richness, and though the centre of the finest rice-growing district in the world, the town is dead. Every thing about it wears an air of dilapidation.*

The day after he had arrived in Georgetown, Gilmore rode north in a buggy driven by a hired slave. After crossing the Black River, he said, "We soon left the region of the rice-fields and plunged into dense forests of the long-leafed pine, where for miles not a house or any other evidence of human occupation is to be seen."

When Gilmore finally arrived at Henry Buck's plantation at the end of the day, he wrote:

> *While emerging from the pine forest, over whose sandy barrens we'd ridden all day, a broad plantation lay spread before us. On one side was a row of perhaps forty small but neat cabins; on the other, at the distance of about a third of a mile, a huge building, which, from the piles of timber near it, I saw was a lumber mill.*

Gilmore stayed overnight at Henry Buck's house and participated in a heated argument with another guest, Robert F.W. Allston, one of the most powerful of all rice-planting Secessionists. Allston declared, "The Union, sir, does not exist. Buchanan has now no more right to quarter a soldier in South Carolina than I have to march an armed force on to the Boston Common. If he persists in keeping troops near Charleston, we shall discharge them." Henry Buck replied, "But that would make war! And war, Colonel, would be a terrible thing. Do you realize what that would bring upon us? And what could our little State do in a conflict with nearly thirty million?" Allston replied that he did not think that the North would fight, saying, "The Democratic party sympathizes with us, and some of its influential leaders are pledged to our side. They will sow division there and paralyze the Free States; besides, the trading and manufacturing classes will never consent to a war that will work their ruin. With the Yankee, sir, the dollar is almighty."

On a rooftop in Charleston on April 12, 1861, brilliant thirty-seven-year-old Charleston socialite Mary Boykin Chesnut watched as the first cannon shots of the Civil War were fired. Her Confederate politician husband, James, had rowed out to Fort Sumter to try and negotiate peace with the

Union commander, Major Robert Anderson. In her diary of that date, Mary Chesnut wrote:

> These long hours the regular sound of cannon roar—men and women rush—prayers—imprecations. What scenes. To night a force will attempt to land. The Harriet Lane has attempted to get in—been shot—her wheel house ruined and she has put to sea. Proud Carolinians—you must conquer on your own soil. The enemy must not land.

One account stated that the bombardment of Fort Sumter could be distinctly heard at Henry Buck's mills, although they were over seventy miles away from Charleston. Buck's brig *Waccamaw* had arrived in Bucksville with William Buck, his young bride, Desiah, and the wedding party in December 1860, just a week before South Carolina seceded from the Union. As the Civil War began, there couldn't have been more contrast between the feelings of newly arrived twenty-two-year old, small-town Yankee girl Desiah McGilvery Buck and the world-wise southern belle, Mary Chesnut. Besides both being beautiful women, they probably wouldn't have found much to agree about. One wonders whether Desiah might not have wanted to re-board the *Waccamaw* and return to Maine.

When the first shots of the Civil War were fired, several of the Maine families, who had moved to Bucksville to work at Henry Buck's mills, struggled to go back to the North. The *Waccamaw* and four other Maine vessels quickly got underway to escape a Confederate blockade. The captain of the *Waccamaw* was James N. Nickels, and his brother, William Sewell Nickels, was first officer. The *Waccamaw* sailed from Bucksville to the Caribbean island of St. Thomas, arriving on June 7, flying the Rebel flag. From there, she sailed directly to Searsport, Maine, and became the first and only vessel during the Civil War to arrive there flying the Confederate flag. William McGilvery quickly had the *Waccamaw* registered as a Maine vessel, after which she sailed for Buenos Aires. All during the Civil War, as long as she wasn't carrying cargo, she was allowed to visit the North and South, flying the appropriate flag. In 1862, W.S. Nickels assumed command of the *Waccamaw* and remained her captain until she went aground and sank near Vera Cruz in 1866.

Another Maine brig, the *B.K. Eaton*, which was partially owned by William McGilvery, was captured by a Confederate privateer in 1861. The crew was jailed in Charleston and then in Columbia. The captain of the *B.K. Eaton*, W.C. Nickels, wrote to William McGilvery several times requesting help in obtaining an exchange of prisoners, which finally occurred in May 1862. Captain Nickels was among many members of that same Searsport family, the Nickels/Nichols, who intermarried with the Buck and McGilvery families, and he commanded sailing vessels throughout the nineteenth century. W.C. Nickels continued to command ships after the Civil War. In 1880, as captain of the *Resolute*, he was captured by mutineers aboard his ship. Still in irons, he escaped, jumped overboard and drowned.

Henry Buck paid heavily for his opposition to secession. He was assessed over $40,000 by the Confederate government. His mills could no longer ship lumber to the North. His son William continued to run the Bucksville mill, supplying lumber for use by the Confederacy. In the North, the ships that Henry Buck owned were confiscated by the Union for its own use. Two of his sons enlisted in the Confederate army. One, George Olney, died of pneumonia while on duty near Charleston in 1865. The other, Captain Henry L. Buck, was captured at Petersburg and later released. A son-in-law, Captain Cephas Gilbert, was commanding officer of a Confederate navy ship that was being built far up the Pee Dee River late during the war. The *Pee Dee* was never completed and was blown up to keep it from falling into the hands of the enemy.

At the end of the war, in 1865, 600,000 lives later, much of the South was in ruins. When some of the 18,000 emancipated slaves of the Georgetown district rampaged through their former owners' plantation homes along the Waccamaw, Henry Buck supported a request by plantation owners for the Federal gunboat *Mingoe* to make a show of force along the river as far up as Conwayborough. When the situation calmed down, Buck, whose wealth had fallen from $1 million to $1,000, recovered quickly. He had maintained his contacts in the North, and pine lumber for ships was much in demand. He restarted his mills and hired many of his emancipated slaves to work for wages. He gave the Negro workers land for their houses and farms. His treatment of the Negroes led to their referring to Bucksville as "Utopia." With help from his sons—William managing the Bucksville mill and Henry Lee the Bucksport mill—all three mills were running, and ships were sailing in and out of Bucksville, loaded with lumber and naval stores, just as before the war. Advertising for vessels to haul lumber from Bucksville, a freight agent in Charleston wrote, "Bucksville to New York 140 to 150 M resawed, the longest of which is 60 to 65 feet long." The agent was seeking a vessel to haul 150,000 board feet[5] of timbers that were as much as 65 feet long.

---

5. A board foot is a measure of lumber volume equal to a timber one foot long, one foot wide and one inch thick.

The rice industry did not recover after the war. Many of the emancipated slaves refused to sign contracts with their former owners to work in the rice fields and to do the hard labor of repairing muddy dikes. The crops of 1865–67 were failures. Acreage of rice in Georgetown County dropped from forty-six thousand in 1860 to sixteen thousand in the 1870s. Many of the planters went bankrupt or lost their land for non-payment of taxes. The "old and refined society" of the rice-planting gentry was gone.

William McGilvery continued to build ships even during the Civil War. In 1863, he built the 125-foot, 421-ton bark *Desiah*, named after his daughter. After the war, in 1870, he built the *Alice Buck*, named for the youngest daughter of Henry and Frances Buck. In 1867, the 125-foot, 683-ton bark *Hudson* was built in Bucksport, Maine, for R.P. Buck of New York and Henry Buck. Henry Buck soon became as wealthy as he had been before the war.

Following an 1867 federal law that gave blacks the right to vote, the South Carolina legislature became dominated by Republicans, composed of emancipated slaves and northern whites who had recently moved to South Carolina. At the age of sixty-eight, Henry Buck ran for and was elected to the state Senate as a Democrat, defeating a black Methodist minister. He voted consistently (but unsuccessfully) against what he saw as corruption and chaos in the state legislature. He hoped, along with the few other Democrats, that the state would be returned to white southern rule. He remained in the Senate until his death in 1870 in Saratoga, New York, where he had gone for treatment of an illness. His body was brought back to Bucksville and buried in the Buck cemetery, across from Hebron Church. An obituary in the October 13, 1870 *San Francisco Bulletin* read:

> *Mr. Buck passed his summers at the North, and was almost as well known in this city and at Saratoga as he was at home. He was a genial and courtly gentleman, and in spite of his Northern birth exhibited most of the characteristic traits of the wealthy Southern planter. Aversion to politics kept him out of public affairs during the larger part of his life, but a few years ago, he consented to serve his fellow-citizens, and at the time of his death, he was the most conspicuous of the five Democratic members of the South Carolina Senate.*

William L. Buck took over management of the mills from his father. He and Desiah lived in the Upper Mill house, where Desiah educated their children with the help of a teacher, Sarah Delano, imported from Maine. William Buck was a man of intelligence and ability, but some said he lacked Henry Buck's ambition. In 1871, he entered into a partnership with C.F. Buck, B.L. Beaty and James

The gravestone of Henry Buck (1801–1870), located in the Buck cemetery across from Hebron Methodist Church. *Photo by Mary McAlister.*

Dusenbury to manufacture and ship pine lumber from Greenwood Steam Sawmills at Bucksville. This sawmill was the largest in the state at that time. In 1874, part of the Bucksville sawmill burned, with uninsured losses of $30,000. At that time, the partnership was dissolved, and William Buck continued the business as W.L. Buck and Company. However, he never dominated the lumber industry as his father had.

In December 1870, less than a year after Henry Buck's death, the brig *E.F. Dunbar* sailed from Searsport to Bucksville to load lumber for the West Indies. She had been built in Searsport by William McGilvery and was commanded by Captain William Sewall Nickels, whose family was aboard for that voyage. The Nickels, Buck and McGilvery families were all friends and relatives, so they had a pleasant visit while the lumber was being loaded in Bucksville. On January 19, 1871, the *E.F. Dunbar* was towed down the Waccamaw River to Georgetown, spent one night there and was towed through Winyah Bay and out to sea. On the night of January 21, she was accidentally rammed by the bark-rigged steamship *Tennessee*. As she was sinking, the schooner *Joseph Segar* came alongside, rescued the passengers and crew and took them back to Georgetown. The abandoned wreck was kept afloat by the buoyancy of her cargo and continued to drift north in the Gulf Stream. She was reported by the ship *W.G. Russell* on February 2 off Cape Hatteras:

Passed close to the wreck of the brig E.F. Dunbar, *waterlogged and abandoned, with fore mast standing and fore yard across bowsprit and main mast gone.*

During the many years of the lumber sailing ship era, several lumber-loaded storm-wrecked vessels, some with their crews still aboard, drifted northward and eastward in the Gulf Stream to as far away as the Azores Islands before sinking into the deep.

Chapter 4
The Legacy of the *Henrietta* and Northeastern Shipbuilding

In 1872, William Buck's father-in-law, Captain William McGilvery, conceived a plan to avoid the expense of shipping lumber from South Carolina to Searsport, Maine, to build ships. He also hoped to avoid another problem faced by the shipbuilders of the Penobscot River. The Penobscot River as far up as Searsport and Bucksport was not deep enough at low tide to launch the largest ships being demanded by owners for worldwide trade. Rather than relocate his shipyard to the deeper Kennebec River, as some shipbuilders did, McGilvery decided to experiment with building a ship near William Buck's lumber mill in Bucksville, South Carolina, the source of most shipbuilding lumber. He would overcome the shortage of skilled shipbuilding labor in Bucksville by sending men from Maine to build the ship. He and William Buck believed that it would be less expensive to build ships in South Carolina, where the pine trees grew, than to ship the materials to Maine. To begin the experiment, McGilvery sent Searsport master shipwright Elisha Dunbar (after whom the brig *E.F. Dunbar* had been named) and sixty additional skilled Searsport shipwrights to Bucksville to build a 115-foot-long, 240-ton schooner to be named *Hattie McGilvery Buck*, after a daughter of William and Desiah Buck. The *Hattie Buck* was quickly built and launched in 1873. The venture was a success, and the *Hattie Buck*, registered in Georgetown, began to carry cargo from Bucksville to the Northeast.

Soon after the launching of the *Hattie Buck*, a travel-adventure writer from Massachusetts, Nathaniel Bishop, paddled a canoe from Quebec to the Gulf of Mexico. He later published a book about the trip titled *Voyage of the Paper Canoe*. Paddling down the Waccamaw River on January 18, 1874, he wrote:

> *The great wilderness was traversed thirty miles to the country town of Conwayborough, where the negroes roared with laughter at the working of the double paddle, as I shot past the landing-place where cotton and naval stores were piled, waiting to be lightered nine miles to Pot Bluff—so called from the fact of a pot being lost from a vessel near it—which place is reached by vessels from New York drawing twelve feet of water. Though still a long distance from the ocean, I was beginning to feel its tidal influences. At Pot Bluff, the landing and comfortable home of its owner, Mr. Z.W. Dusenbury, presented a pleasant relief after the monotony of the great pine forests.*

The next day, Bishop paddled down the river, passing Bucksville, where the *Hattie Buck* had been launched, past Tip Top Plantation, through Bull Creek and up the Pee Dee River to the home of Mr. M.L. Blakely of New York, who was engaged in the manufacture of cypress shingles. Bishop wrote:

> *A loud halloo greeted me from the swamp, where a party of negro shingle makers were at work. They manned their boat, a long cypress dug-out, and followed me. Their employer, who proved to be a gentleman, whose abiding-place I was now rapidly approaching, sat in the stern. We landed together before the old plantation house, which had been occupied a few years before by members of the wealthy and powerful rice-planting aristocracy of the Pee Dee but was now the temporary home of a*

Captain Jonathan C. Nickels, managing owner and first master of the ship *Henrietta*. *Courtesy of Penobscot Marine Museum.*

Drawing by S.S. Stevens of a two-masted schooner being towed past Bucksville while the *Henrietta* is under construction in 1875. *Courtesy of Penobscot Marine Museum.*

northern man, who was busily employed in guiding the labors of his four hundred freedmen in the swamps of North and South Carolina.

Based on the success of the *Hattie Buck*, William McGilvery and a retired Searsport master mariner and shipbuilder, Captain Jonathan C. Nickels, decided to build a much larger vessel in Bucksville: a two-hundred-foot-long, 1,200-ton, square-rigged ship known as a Downeaster. Downeasters were designed for the California grain trade, and these magnificent ships were world renowned for smartness in appearance and handling. They were the epitome of square-rigged sailing ships. They were almost as fast as earlier clipper ships[6] and could carry more cargo. More than two hundred Downeasters were launched from many New England shipyards, including those in Bath, Thomaston, East Boston, Newburyport, Mystic, Rockport, Rockland and Searsport. The famous maritime historian Howard I. Chapelle, speaking of Maine Downeasters, said:

6. Both clipper ships and Downeasters were square-rigged ships, meaning that all masts had square sails and yardarms, horizontal timbers that supported the square sails. Clipper ships were reported to be the fastest square-riggers ever built.

The part of the Maine shipbuilders and designers in the history of American sailing ships has never received full recognition. The so-called Downeasters that followed the clipper were almost wholly the work of these men. Some of the vessels were, without doubt, the highest development of the sailing-ship; combining speed, handiness, cargo-capacity and low operating costs to a degree never obtained in any earlier square-rigger.

The Downeaster that Nickels and McGilvery proposed to build in Bucksville, South Carolina, would be the first and only Downeaster ever built in the South and would be the largest wooden sailing ship ever built in South Carolina. The citizens of Bucksville were excited about the prospects of shipbuilding in their community. The owners and financers of the ship were convinced that she could be built for less money than an equivalent ship built in the Northeast. The owners of shares in the ship were almost all relatives of Nickels, Buck or McGilvery. They were J.C. Nickels, William McGilvery, T.H. Buck, A.V. Nickels, Lizzie McGilvery Nickels, H.K. Nickels, E.D. Blanchard, William L. Buck, Desiah McGilvery Buck, Mary J. Sarvis, Alice Buck, Lucinda Gilbeth, H. Kaminski, A.K. Thompson, A.J. Ross and Hoodson and Plummer. The ship would be named the *Henrietta*, after the wife of Jonathan Nickels, principal owner of the ship. A Belfast, Maine newspaper reported on October 10, 1874:

Searsport Captain McGilvery is to try the experiment of building a ship at Bucksville, S.C. Some of the men have already gone forward, 60 workmen in all, and will come from different places along the Penobscot. The work is to be under the direction of master-builder Elisha Dunbar of Searsport.

Elisha Dunbar was an experienced master shipbuilder who had been in charge of building many ships in Searsport, both for William McGilvery and Jonathan Nickels. He had just completed the 240-ton schooner *Hattie Buck* in Bucksville the year before. This next ship was to be a much larger project, and Dunbar knew the kind of men and the number it would take to build her. He was able to convince those he wanted to take by telling them that they would be living in warm South Carolina during the winter months, when Maine weather was too cold to build. He selected the men he needed and gathered iron, cordage and other

The original registry of the *Henrietta*, 1875. *Courtesy of Penobscot Marine Museum.*

materials and tools that he knew wouldn't be available in that isolated part of the world. Jonathan Nickels and William McGilvery agreed to relocate almost their entire shipyards from Searsport to Bucksville. In all, 115 ship's carpenters, riggers, joiners, caulkers, blacksmiths and other specialists moved to Bucksville to built the 1,200-ton ship *Henrietta*.

Bucksville had a population of several hundred, but the addition of 115 shipyard workers would place a strain on the ability of the community to take care of them. Most of the men who came down from Searsport had never been to South Carolina. A few had crewed on Searsport ships that had loaded lumber in Bucksville. A few more had been south as Union soldiers. They knew they were going into a strange land, but it was their chance to work and make money during the winter. The local Bucksville population, except for a few transplanted Maine northerners, was made up of poor southern white farmers and millworkers, many of whom had fought for the Confederacy during the Civil War, which had been over for only ten years. Emancipated slaves made up the remainder of the population of Bucksville. It would be an alien environment for the Maine shipwrights. The men said goodbye to their families and arrived in Bucksville in September 1874, when the weather was still hot in South Carolina. Most of them had never encountered southern heat, humidity, insects, snakes and alligators. William Buck tried to make the men comfortable but without much success. They had often worked for Elisha Dunbar but never under these conditions. They slept in camp-like barracks, ate strange local foods and had little to do except work. Several of the workers became sick from the "miasma" in the air and were returned to their homes in Maine. It was no wonder that there was disgruntlement among the workers. It was miraculous that they managed to prepare the slipway and lay the massive keel of the ship in the fall heat and humidity, which was soon followed by an unusually severe winter.

The men from Maine and ten or fifteen laborers from South Carolina, who William Buck had supplied, worked together in the swamps along the river to find and cut suitable trees. It took 1.3 million feet of mill-cut lumber, mostly longleaf pine, to build the *Henrietta*. Elisha Dunbar, assisted by master builder Jerome Stevens, might have used a small-scale half-model of the vessel, which he would have carved in Maine, to lay out full-scale patterns of the frames on a rough lofting floor. The stem, sternpost, breast hooks, knees and some other parts of the structure were built of oak. The remainder of the hull structure, including the frames, was built of longleaf pine. Almost all of the work, with the exception of sawing out sections of frames with the steam-powered saws from the lumber mill, had to be done in the open by hand. Frames were fastened together with oak treenails and iron spikes. The men worked from sunup to sundown, six days a week, throughout the cold drizzly winter, shaping the structure of the bow and stern and raising frames into place. As the frames were tilted upright by block and tackle, their tops extended more than forty feet above the river, higher than anything else in the little village behind the ship. When the 200-foot-long ship was framed up, she looked like a cathedral. Steamboats

Drawing by S.S. Stevens of a tug chugging up the Waccamaw River past the *Henrietta* while under construction. The cabins have been built, and she is almost ready to be launched. *Courtesy of Penobscot Marine Museum.*

and flats, passing Bucksville on their way to and from Georgetown, gawked at the huge structure rising on the riverbank.

Once the framing and deck beams were installed, a massive oak-and-pine keelson was built on top of the keel, from bow to stern, to strengthen the backbone of the vessel. Hard pine exterior planking and interior ceilings were sawn, steamed, wedged and spiked to the frames to complete the hull structure. Lifting equipment was primitive compared to shipyards in Maine. Beams and decking were dragged up ramps or lifted by block and tackle. Framing around holes for hatches, masts and other openings was completed, and pine decks were spiked down. Seams between planking and decking timbers were filled with oakum and cotton, pounded in and sealed with pitch. Two large cabins, the forecastle and the aft cabin, were built on top of the deck. J.A. McPhail of Boston was in charge of the joiners who did the finish work in the cabins. A newspaper writer, upon visiting the ship, observed, "The men used wood and trimmings from the North in the after cabin. The front cabin is finished with cedar, pine and walnut sawed and manufactured at Bucksville, and the contrast between the two cabins is decidedly in favor of the Southern finish." Fixtures, furnishings and equipment for the ship were built. Anchors, chain and a capstan windlass were installed.[7] Nicholas Roberts of Searsport and E.S. Walker of Yarmouth "cut up, wrought and riveted in the ship over 65 tons of iron." It took almost eight months to build the ship. Although they had brought a supply of iron, cordage and other materials and tools from Maine, there were shortages, which caused delays. The *Henrietta* was completed, with the exception of masts and rigging, in April 1875. She was 201 feet long, 39 feet wide, 24 feet deep when loaded and 13 feet deep as launched.

The men building the *Henrietta* were relieved to see a beautiful spring. They had learned to enjoy hunting and fishing during their little bits of time off from work. Some had made friends with local people while attending Sunday services at Hebron Methodist Church. They began to see why living in the South might not be so bad and why some people from Maine had permanently moved to Bucksville. A few of the single men decided to stay in South Carolina, but most of the men longed to go home to their families.

Charles Dusenbury, who observed the *Henrietta* under construction and who was present at her launching into the Waccamaw River on April 29, 1875, noted:

> *The cabin was built of longleaf pine and was one of the most attractive pieces of workmanship of that kind that I ever saw. The launching was a gala event. There were five steamboats there, all loaded with people, and people came in every conceivable vehicle, I would say, from fifty miles around. That night, we took two headlights out of the mill and put one in each end of the ship, between decks, which brightly lighted it. We had a string band from Georgetown, and the young folks at Bucksville, with those who remained over the night, danced about all night. Unlike some launchings, everything happened as it should have. As the crowd watched from boat and bank, Master Dunbar knocked out the wedge which held the* Henrietta *in place on the ways. This wedge loosened everything, and the ship left the land, and with all ease and grace, she stepped into her new home—the water.*

The *Henrietta* was launched with her masts and rigging lying on her deck. There were too many trees overhanging the river to try to step the masts before launching the ship. Drawing thirteen feet of water, she was towed by a steam tugboat down the Waccamaw River to Georgetown,

---

7. A capstan is an apparatus that enabled the anchor to be raised by hand. A windlass is a horizontal cylinder, turned by a capstan, to make raising the anchor less difficult. Oakum is loose hemp or jute fibers, made from old rope, used to seal the spaces between planks.

A painting by Charles Patterson of the *Henrietta* under sail. *Courtesy of Penobscot Marine Museum.*

bumping along the bottom. It was well known that some spots in Winyah Bay were only twelve feet deep at high tide. Charles Dusenbury described how the *Henrietta* reached the Atlantic:

> *They built what they called a cradle. It was a network of ropes holding two hundred empty spirits of turpentine barrels which they put under the ship and raised her up. They filled the barrels with water and put them in place, then pumped the water out and bunged the barrels up, and they did the work. They had lines across the ship, and one fastened to the bow, and when they got into deep sea, they let go the lines and the tug that towed her to sea picked up the cradle and towed it back to town. The barrels were as good as ever.*

The *Henrietta* was towed to Charleston, where her three masts were stepped and all of the spars and rigging installed, all within a month. Captain Pendleton of Searsport supervised the rigging of the ship. A Bostonian, G.W. Putnam, was charged with securing the masts and spars. Two sets of twenty-four sails each were delivered from Boston. She carried a skysail on her mainmast, whose topmast towered 147 feet above the deck. The *Henrietta* was prepared for sea and sailed in June 1875 for St. John, New Brunswick, Canada, with Captain Jonathan Nickels in command of a crew of twenty-five men. From there, with his wife aboard, he sailed to Liverpool and back to St. John. During the return voyage, Captain Nickels on the *Henrietta* won a race against his brother, commanding the ship *Lucy A. Nickels* (named after Jonathan Nickels's first wife, who had died). Captain Jonathan Nickels declared the maiden voyage a success. Throughout her career, the *Henrietta* was known as a fast and reliable ship.

Jonathan Nickels, William McGilvery, William Buck and the citizens of Bucksville, South Carolina, claimed that the *Henrietta* had been a financial success. W.L. Buck and Company declared that the *Henrietta* had cost a total of $77,368.06, "including her top bills and expenses from Bucksville to St. Johns." A similar but somewhat larger ship, the *Brown Brothers*, was built in Newburyport, Massachusetts, in 1875 by Captain Daniel Goodell, an ex-partner of William McGilvery, for a cost of $115,000.00. The *New York Bulletin* and other northern newspapers claimed that the *Henrietta* had cost $65.00 per ton and that ships in the North were being built for $60.00 per ton. Nickels, McGilvery and Buck said that the *Henrietta* had cost $61.06 per ton, 10 percent less than northern ships. They also said that they intended to build another ship at Bucksville. In the end, no more ships were built there. Charles Dusenbury was probably correct when he stated:

Captain William McGilvery was a Searsport, Maine shipbuilder and part owner of the *Henrietta*. *Courtesy of Penobscot Marine Museum.*

Ninety percent of W.L. Buck and Company's business was with ship builders of the North, and they to a man notified W.L. Buck and Co. that if they continued shipbuilding at Bucksville, they [the northern shipbuilders] *would do no more business with them. After due consideration, W.L. Buck and Co. decided that the Northern trade was worth the most.*

FOR SALE TO CLOSE AN ESTATE.

Will be sold at Public Auction, (if not previously sold at private sale, at

Union Hall, Searsport, the 18th day of September, A. D. 1878, at 10 o'clock A. M.,

all the Personal Property then belonging to the estate of WILLIAM McGILVERY, late of Searsport, deceased, per following list and description:

VESSELS.

Interest.	Rig.	Name.	Tons.	Built.	Amr'n.	French.	When Metaled.
1-8	Ship	Mary Goodell,	761	1854	A1½	5 6 1 1	1878, July.
1-16	"	David Brown,	905	1884	A1		1876, January.
5-32	"	J. C. Potter,	1244	1869	"	3 3 1 1	1876
7-64	"	Henrietta,	1207	1875	"	"	1877, September.
7-64	"	Premier,	1393	1875	"	"	1876,
1-16	"	Susan Gilmore,	1204	1874	"	"	1876
1-32	"	Nancy Pendleton,	1449	1872	"	"	1877, January.
1-32	"	Frank Pendleton,	1414	1874	"	"	1877, November.
5-16	Bark	Com. Dupont,	434	1862	A1½	5 6 1 1	1875, October.
1-8	"	Anna Walsh,	575	1864	"		1874, "
1-8	"	Robert Porter,	840	1865	A1½		1876, August.
1-8	"	Herbert Black,	573	1873	A1	3 3 1 1	1875.
1-32	"	S. E. Kingsbury,	506	1869	"		1875, December.
1-8	"	Aberdeen,	321	1856	A1½	5 6 1 1	1876, September.
1-8	"	Arletta,	373	1864	A1½	"	1877, March.
1-8	"	C. A. Littlefield,	548	1864	"		1877, August.
1-16	"	Mary E. Russell,	575	1875	A1	3 3 1 1	1876.
1-4	"	Beatrice Havener,	553	1875	"	"	1877, March.
9-32	"	Fred W. Carlon,	531	1875	"	"	1878, June.
7-32	Barkentine	Clara E. McGilvery,	402	1873	"		1878, July.
1-8	Brig	Liberty,	290	1866	A1½		1877, September.
1-16	"	Clytie,	369	1866	"		1878, July.
5-16	"	Manson,	264	1867	A1½		1877, September.
1-16	"	J. H. Lane,	391	1869	A1		1877, "
1-16	Schooner	Brunette,	86	1871	A1½		none.
1-16	"	Lizzie Lane,	231	1874	A1½		"
1-32	"	Thomas W. Holder,	231	1875			"

6 Shares Portland & Machias Steamboat Company Stock.

20 Shares Bangor & Piscataquis R. R. Company Stock.

20 Shares Danver Carpet Company Stock.

1 Share in "Maine Lloyds" of Bangor, Me.

1 Large Office Safe, Marvin's patent and manufacture—made in 1875.

3 Office Desks and lot of Office Furniture.

15 Clamp Screws.

1 Ship Yard Capstain.

3 Jackscrews.

1 Treenail Machine.

2 Mast Blocks.

4 Cross Cut Saws.

1 Whip Saw.

1 Set Hard Pine Launching Ways, in 18 large pieces.

1 Bolt Cutter.

142 tons Oak Timber.

122 Spruce Knees.

1 M. Spruce Lumber.

2 Plows.

1 Pung.

All the outstanding notes and accounts belonging to the Estate and amounting to about $20,000 and worth about $3000.

Also at the same time and place, by virtue of a license from the Probate Court, the reversion of the widow's dower in the following named Real Estate, viz:

One undivided half of the J. H. Lane store in Searsport—a fine, large, three-story building, well rented—and land connected with same.

The Benj. Colcord Place, so called, in Searsport Village—a large, two story house and ell, with wood sheds, barn and about seven acres of land.

One undivided eighth part of the Methodist Parsonage House and lot in Searsport Village—a good two story house, with ell, barn and a small lot of land, well rented.

Sundry pews in Methodist Church in Searsport.

Pew No. 71 in " " " Belfast.

Also, on the premises in Brewer, Maine, on

Thursday, the 19th day of September next,

At 11 o'clock A. M., the Marine Railways and Ship Yard, formerly occupied by Wm. McGilvery & Co. together with the reversion of the widow's dower therein.

TERMS CASH.

WILLIAM L. BUCK, } Administrators of Estate of William McGilvery.
HENRY H. GRANT, }

A listing of the 1876 estate of Captain William McGilvery. His son-in-law, William Buck, was an administrator of the estate. *Courtesy of Monica Pattangall.*

Despite his satisfaction with the *Henrietta's* sailing ability, Captain Nickels decided not to build additional ships in South Carolina. It was reported that he said the expense of transporting and maintaining New England workmen so far from home, in addition to other possible inconveniences of climate, depth of channel and furnishing of supplies, was greater than anticipated. Captain Nickels returned to Searsport and, with master builder Elisha Dunbar in charge, built his next and last ship, the *R.R. Thomas*. At 202 feet by 40 feet by 24 feet

A painting of the *Henrietta* sailing at night. *Courtesy of Penobscot Marine Museum.*

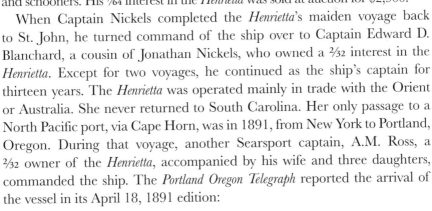

Captain A.M. Ross, the last captain of the *Henrietta. Courtesy of Penobscot Marine Museum.*

and 1,333 tons, she was almost the same size as the *Henrietta.* Jonathan Nickels lived the rest of his life in Searsport and died there in 1889.

Captain William M. McGilvery built no more ships. He committed suicide on March 9, 1876. His reasons might have included the stress of the *Henrietta* experiment, but the primary cause was his grief over the loss of his youngest daughter while on her honeymoon aboard ship less than a year before. William McGilvery was mourned by all of the citizens of Searsport. His son-in-law, William Buck, was one of the administrators of his substantial estate, which included partial ownership of twenty-six barks, brigs and schooners. His 7/64 interest in the *Henrietta* was sold at auction for $2,900.

When Captain Nickels completed the *Henrietta*'s maiden voyage back to St. John, he turned command of the ship over to Captain Edward D. Blanchard, a cousin of Jonathan Nickels, who owned a 2/32 interest in the *Henrietta*. Except for two voyages, he continued as the ship's captain for thirteen years. The *Henrietta* was operated mainly in trade with the Orient or Australia. She never returned to South Carolina. Her only passage to a North Pacific port, via Cape Horn, was in 1891, from New York to Portland, Oregon. During that voyage, another Searsport captain, A.M. Ross, a 2/32 owner of the *Henrietta*, accompanied by his wife and three daughters, commanded the ship. The *Portland Oregon Telegraph* reported the arrival of the vessel in its April 18, 1891 edition:

REMARKABLY STAUNCH

Though the foreign ships arriving here are generally good vessels with agreeable captains, it is with pardonable pride when an opportunity is offered to chronicle the arrival of a ship which flies the starry emblem of liberty. That is afforded now, for the American ship Henrietta, *Captain A.M. Ross, arrived yesterday afternoon and is now at the wharf foot of B*

Street, discharging cargo. Her registered tonnage is 1,203, but she carries 1,800 tons, drawing 22 feet when loaded. She has two decks, 24 sails, a crew of 20 men and carries three boats.

RECORD OF HER LOG

She left New York on the first of last November, was 106 days reaching Cape Horn, and 56 days from there to the Columbia River bar. Of that time, 36 days were occupied in going from 50 degrees south latitude on the Atlantic, around to the same latitude on the Pacific. Head winds were continually encountered and the ship obliged to turn about and go back. The gales from the westward were terrific, often accompanied by sleet and hail. Three times Cape Horn was east and north, and six times it was sighted. The progress on the Atlantic was very slow, no favorable trade winds being encountered, though the ship bore far to the eastward searching for them.

WELL-EQUIPPED RIGGING

The original fore and main masts have been replaced by new ones, the lower being both of iron. One was put in at Singapore and the other at Melbourne. The rigging and the entire ship presents a fine appearance, everything being in good order, and an air of neatness is plainly apparent all over the vessel. Captain Ross is part owner and gives his best efforts to keep the ship in perfect condition so that even if it is fifteen years old, it seems more like a new ship. The wheel is covered with a comfortable house, the forecastle is commodious, the galley large and convenient and supplied with a large range and an abundance of cooking utensils.

A HOME-LIKE APPEARANCE

The cabin is large with comfortable staterooms, and as the captain has his family with him, it presents a home-like appearance in agreeable contrast to the dingy air of loneliness which pervades the cabin where no woman lives. Mrs. Ross and her three youngest daughters came on the ship and stood the voyage excellently. One is 9, another 8, and the youngest 4 years of age, all girls, and the oldest daughter is at school in Searsport, ME, with her grandparents. The daughter 8 years of age is named Henrietta, both she and the ship being named for the same lady in Maine.

Family Matters

Mrs. Ross is a lady of fine appearance, pleasing manners, well educated and quite interesting in conversation. She is the daughter of an old sea captain and, when a girl, made many voyages with her father. This is her first long voyage after several years, but she is never seasick and not easily frightened. She feels as much at home on the bounding billow as when on shore. Flowers, music, books, pictures and home adornments attest the refinement and culture of Mrs. Ross and give the cabin and staterooms an air of neatness and good taste which is decidedly attractive.

This newspaper article doesn't tell the whole story of life at sea for the typical crewman on a square-rigged, deep-water sailing ship. The wooden merchant sailing ship—especially a fast vessel—was probably the most dangerous vehicle ever used on a large scale. Many men were lost in ships that simply disappeared between ports, being overwhelmed by stress of weather, foundering after springing a leak or even catching fire and burning to the waterline. Frequently, merchant seamen would be away from home for three years or more. For months, the seaman was isolated from the rest of mankind and all womankind in a community comprising a dozen or so inmates of the forecastle in which he lived. The forecastle of the deep-water square-rigger was often damp and unheated and sometimes could be a floating slum. The seaman worked no fewer than eighty-four hours per week and rarely had more than four hours' sleep at a time. The work was difficult and dangerous, the food was usually bad and the pay was low. By 1891, it was difficult for a captain to find competent and experienced crew. Few men other than those who couldn't find work ashore or on steamships would agree to serve on a square-rigged sailing ship. Once ashore in some port away from home, such as Portland, a typical sailor would quickly spend all he had earned on booze and women.

During the *Henrietta*'s stay in Portland, she was visited by President Benjamin Harrison, who took much interest in her. After leaving Portland, the *Henrietta* sailed to Melbourne, Australia, and from there around the Cape of Good Hope to Boston. The world-circumnavigation voyage took about eighteen months. Captain Ross continued to command the *Henrietta*, but his wife and children stayed behind in Searsport. From Boston, the ship loaded lumber for Buenos Aires, a trip that would take forty-nine days. From Buenos Aires, she returned to New York in ballast in forty-five days. In New York, she loaded oil for Singapore and came back to New York with general cargo, again loading oil for Yokohama.

The crew of a square-rigger, aloft on a yardarm and wrestling with a sail. *Courtesy of Penobscot Marine Museum.*

In August 1894, the *Henrietta* loaded some eight hundred tons of manganese ore and crockery at Yokohama, Japan, and proceeded to Kobe to complete her lading for New York. She was overtaken by a typhoon when entering Kobe harbor, and the pilot in charge ran her back some fifteen miles to what was considered a secure anchorage. Captain Ross wrote:

On August 25 at 3 AM glass falling we decided not to get underway. Wind about ENE. At 10 AM blowing heavy gale from ESE, 120 fathoms on starboard (anchor) and 90 on port. At 12:30 PM parted starboard chain forward of windlass—typhoon gusts—gave her all port chain and let go stream anchor with 60 fathoms of manila hawser bent on, and backer on port chain—new 8½-inch manila to foremast. At 4:30 PM port chain parted some 50 or 60 fathoms from hawsepipe—ship then drifting broadside on beach. The stream with hawser went. Still drifting broadside on. Cleared away end of port chain after much difficulty, and just before she struck, got her head on. Tremendous sea running and ship pounding

The hulk of the *Henrietta* before being broken up in Kobe, Japan, in 1894. *Courtesy of the State Library of Victoria, Australia.*

very heavily and consequently soon filled with water—11 feet. At 10:30 PM typhoon subsided and sea following, she soon lay quiet. With 6 feet water forward at low well and about [illegible] *aft at low, ship seemed to be bearing the burden in wake of fore rigging. I proceed to Kobe as soon as possible. Consulted with Orvil. Held survey which resulted, as reported in survey, the sale of same, following at earliest possible date at public auction.*

All hands from the ship had been landed safely and made their way back to Searsport. Captain Ross retired from the sea to make his home in Searsport and become one of the town's most respected citizens. Searsport was home to more ship captains than any other place in the United States.

Because of extensive damage to her hull, the *Henrietta* was condemned and eventually broken up in a yard in Kobe, Japan. All of the pine and oak timbers from the forests of Bucksville, South Carolina, were cut into small pieces and sold in bundles to the citizens of Kobe for use in their stoves and fireplaces.

Many other wooden sailing ships, owned by northerners, spent their working lives hauling lumber and other cargo from the port of Georgetown to the Northeast during the late 1800s and early 1900s. Heiman Kaminski, a prominent Jewish businessman in Georgetown and one of the owners of

Mr. Heiman Kaminski, prominent Georgetown businessman, part owner of the ship *Henrietta* and principal owner of the schooner *Linah C. Kaminski*. *Courtesy of Georgetown County Digital Library.*

the *Henrietta*, was one of the few South Carolinians who had the foresight to acquire his own cargo vessel. In 1882, Kaminski ordered the building of a three-masted schooner (132 by 33 by 14 feet, 421 tons), which he named *Linah C. Kaminski*, after his mother. The schooner was built along the Kennebec River in Bath, Maine, by the Goss and Sawyer shipyard and could carry 300,000 feet of lumber. Several of the other owners of the *Linah C. Kaminski* were also owners of the *Henrietta*, including Desiah Buck, Fannie Buck and several wives of Buck family members. Stephen E. Woodbury of Bucksville was captain of the *Kaminski*.

Woodbury had previously lived in Searsport and had been owner and master of the 117-foot schooner *Stephen E. Woodbury*, built by William McGilvery in 1866. Woodbury operated the *Stephen E. Woodbury* between Maine and Bucksville until 1881, when he sold her. On March 7, 1885, Captain Woodbury, accompanied by his wife and crew, sailed the *Kaminski* out of Georgetown with a cargo of naval stores headed for New York. Captain Woodbury related his story:

We encountered bad weather almost from the beginning of the passage. About 2 a.m. on the third day out, while heading north northwest under close reefed sails, our position being twenty miles off Cape Charles, an alarm signal was given by the watch that a vessel was right ahead. In less time than it takes to tell it, we and the other vessel came together head-on. The other vessel, a three-masted schooner, struck on our port bow, cutting waist and side down from fore to the mizzen rigging to below the deck, taking one

A painting of the three-masted schooner *Linah C. Kaminski. Courtesy of Mr. and Mrs. Michael Prevost.*

wale off in places. As soon as we struck, the other schooner dropped anchor, which separated us, and a minute thereafter, my main and mizzenmasts came down with a crash. I also thought the mainmast of the other schooner came down, as I heard a crash on board her also. While the two vessels were together, my crew of mates, men and steward deserted my vessel and jumped on board the other, leaving myself and my wife alone. I commanded my mate and crew to return to the Kaminski, *but they paid no attention. As soon as we separated, we drifted helplessly away to the eastward. During the whole of that day, I had a lookout for passing vessels. I saw a number of them, but not one bore down on us. One schooner passed so close that I could see men walking on deck, and they must have seen us in our helpless condition, but they made no effort to come near. Mrs. Woodbury was painfully bruised by the force of the collision but bore up wonderfully well during the trying day and night we spent alone on the deck of the* Kaminski. *I tied Mrs. Woodbury to the spanker mast[8] to keep her from being washed overboard. I manned the pumps as best I could through the night. The next day, on Wednesday, a German ship, the* Dakota *from Hamburg, spotted us about 6 a.m. and approached us. I signaled from the deck, and they hove to and*

---

8. The spanker is the mast that is most aft.

sent a lifeboat near us. A heavy sea was running and a gale of wind was blowing, but they took us off. We saved nothing and were exhausted by the time we boarded the Dakota. *Captain Schaeffer brought us into Baltimore. No man could have done more for us than he did.*

As it turned out, the abandoned *Linah C. Kaminski* was towed into Sandy Hook by a fishing vessel, whose owners claimed her as a prize. Heiman Kaminski and the other owners of the *Kaminski* had to pay a hefty price to reclaim ownership and have the vessel repaired. Several years later, when Heiman Kaminski was serving as agent for the Clyde Steamship Line in Georgetown, he succumbed to the realization that steamships could haul twice as much lumber as schooners and could deliver it twice as fast, so he sold his interest in the *Linah C. Kaminski.*

Chapter 5

1885–1900

The Decline of Bucksville and the Buck Family's Lumber Mills

William L. Buck and Co. continued to thrive throughout the 1870s, shipping record loads of lumber to the Northeast. William's brother, Henry Lee, managed the Lower Mill at Bucksport, and together they reached the peak of their lumber output. Lumber from Buck's mills was in demand for shipbuilding in New England, railroad ties in the West and factories and houses in the Northeast. Lumber from a Buck mill was even used in the construction of the Brooklyn Bridge. Bucksville as a community also reached its high point, with a population of seven hundred more than the only other town in the county, Conwayborough, which was renamed Conway. At that time, Bucksville had two schools, a Masonic lodge, a hotel, two churches and a store where mill employees could buy supplies with tokens that were part of their pay.

In 1876, William Buck was elected to the South Carolina Senate as a Democrat. Republicans, composed of emancipated slaves and white scalawags and carpetbaggers, had been in the majority in the state's legislature since the beginning of Reconstruction. At the time of Buck's election, there was much violence and chaos in the state between blacks and whites. The Democratic Party organized itself for the November 1876 election for governor. General Wade Hampton III,[9] a military hero of the Civil War, was the party's choice for governor. Hampton and his Redshirt

---

9. The author of the foreword to this book is the great-great-niece of General Wade Hampton III.

A schooner from Georgetown & Bull Creek, similar to the *Hattie McGilvery Buck*, unloading barrels of naval stores in New York City during the 1870s. The Brooklyn Bridge is under construction in the background. *Courtesy of Georgetown County Digital Library.*

supporters covered the state, drumming up the votes of white Democrats and intimidating black Republicans. The white farmers of the state, who had been drawn into a war that they had not wanted, were poorer than ever and feared that blacks would take what little they had. They overwhelmingly supported Hampton. When the votes for governor were counted, Wade Hampton won by a slim margin. However, the Republican-dominated legislature claimed that there had been election fraud, and it voided the results. William Buck was among those Democrats in the Senate who were on the losing side of an election dispute in the legislature, which led to the inauguration of the Republican candidate for governor. Wade Hampton responded, "The people have elected me Governor, and by the Eternal God, I will be Governor or we shall have a military governor."

For a few months, there were two legislatures and two claimants for governor. Finally, in April 1877, Wade Hampton's forces prevailed. He was declared governor, Reconstruction was over and white political rule returned to South Carolina.

William Buck remained in the Senate until his death in 1880. His obituary read:

> *Mr. Buck had gone to Charleston to receive medical treatment for an internal tumor, which disease caused his death. William L. Buck was a gentleman of intelligence and ability, had many friends, both in the North and the South, and at the time of his death was a member of the South Carolina State Senate. He was 52 years of age and leaves a wife and 7 children.*

William's brother, Henry Lee Buck, took over ownership of the lumber mills. He, his wife and their five children lived at Bucksville. At that time, the lumber mill at Bucksville was probably the largest and best equipped in the state. As late as 1890, six million feet of pine and cypress were cut at Bucksville and four million cypress shingles were made there.

The Buck mills continued to ship lumber to the shipbuilders of Maine to build coastal topsail schooners, designed to haul bulk cargoes, like coal and lumber, up and down the East Coast of the United States. These schooners were among the last wooden sailing ships built in the United States. Over 1,500 of them were built between 1880 and 1910. The shipbuilders still preferred longleaf pine for the planking and decking of these vessels, but they had found sources other than the Bucksville mill from which to acquire it.

An 1891 article about Bucksville appeared in the *Charleston World* newspaper, which stated:

> *The lumber mill is probably the largest and one of the best equipped in the state. The power is generated in a battery of four immense longitudinal boilers, which supply steam to two monster engines, which produce several hundred horsepower. On the first floor of the mill are situated the lath*

machines, trimmers, edgers, shingle machines, etc. On the second floor are the great gang saws, planing machines, turning lathes, butt saws and rip saws. All of the machinery is of modern pattern.

Besides manufacturing lumber, Buck & Co. are merchants, buying all kinds of produce and selling everything that can be desired. Bucksville is a remarkably healthful village. Both air and water are pure as the purest, and only a few miles distant is Cowford Springs, a mineral water that has become famous because of its wonderful medicinal properties. The soil about here is remarkably fertile. Anything will grow. Truck of all kinds springs up and matures almost like Jonah's gourd. Cereals are the standard crops, though considerable cotton is being planted. One of the specialties in farming here is the plantation of Capt. B.L. Beaty, on which he has a pear orchard of some 800 or 900 trees and a tea farm. His tea has attained at least a state notoriety and has demonstrated the fact that tea culture in South Carolina is not a failure. The flavor of the tea is said to be about the same as English breakfast. Mr. W. McG. Buck has also been successful in tobacco culture at this place. In the village, there are two schools, a Masonic lodge and two churches.

Strong efforts, which are likely to be successful, are being made to induce an extension of the Wilmington, Chadbourne and Conway railroad to this place, where a deepwater terminus can be had. Should this be accomplished, it is probable arrangements will be made with the Clyde steamship line to run the Fanita and other steamers which run to Georgetown, up to Bucksville, connecting with the railroad. The projected Norfolk, Wilmington and Charleston Seacoast Shortline will strike this place. Farming lands can be bought here for $2 per acre, but this price is not guaranteed when these roads are completed. And one great advantage farmers have here is that they do not have to buy guano. Marl is to be had for the cost of transportation, and that is no great distance.

Rose Vine Inn, kept by Mrs. C.F. Buck, is one of the institutions of the village which has become absolutely indispensable: nor could another hostelry take its place. First of all, the house is a typical southern home, then a hotel—not that the duties of hostess are neglected for those of housewife, but Mrs. Buck blends the two so admirably that guests almost forget that sordid dollars and cents enter into the consideration. To be entertained at Rose Vine Inn once is to be its friend forever.

To visit Bucksville and note its situation and surroundings is to be impressed with the fact that the future holds for much that is good. As a residence place, situated among the pines and within two hour's drive

Buck's sawmill chimney is all that remains of Bucksville. *Photo by Mary McAlister*.

of the sea, it has no superior for healthfulness; the river affords a natural highway for commerce, and when the railroads come, as they must, numerous diversified pursuits will spring up to the immeasurable benefit of all concerned.

The *World* article was obviously aimed at generating new business for the lumber mill at Bucksville, but it didn't succeed. Competition from lumber mills in Georgetown, Conway and elsewhere began to take its toll. As competition from other lumber mills increased, Henry Lee and William M., the son of William L. Buck, encouraged the people of Bucksville, who were no longer needed at the lumber mill, to farm the land where trees had been cut and to plant cotton, truck products and tobacco. As lumber production dwindled, Bucksville's population declined. In 1892, Henry Lee Buck sold his holdings in Bucksport and returned to the family home at Upper Mill. He continued to operate the mill in Bucksville and was a member of the state Senate until he died in 1904. That same year, the Bucksville lumber mill burned. The mill was not replaced, and the town of Bucksville died with it. There is nothing left of the town of Bucksville except for the sawmill's brick chimney, surrounded by woods.

The mill at Bucksport continued to operate. In 1899, Mr. D.V. Richardson, who married a daughter of Henry Lee Buck, bought the lumber mill at Bucksport and operated it as a cypress shingle mill. For a number of years, he chartered the schooner *Bayard Hopkins* to load shingles in Bucksport for delivery to New York and Boston. His mill burned in 1918. Lumbering, naval stores and the manufacture of cypress shingles continued at Bucksport and Conway well into the twentieth century. During the 1920s, New York financier Simeon Chapin bought half interest in the timberlands of Burroughs and Collins east of Conway and began the development of a coastal resort that would become Myrtle Beach. A U.S. Coast Guard station was located at Bucksport during World War II. An Intracoastal Waterway pleasure marina still operates there.

The Buck family mills had been the largest lumbering operation in coastal South Carolina from 1840 until 1885. As the Buck lumber industry declined after 1885, several of the Bucks and other transplanted Maine families moved away from Bucksville and Bucksport to find work in Georgetown, Conway or elsewhere. Some white farmers and many black farmers continued to live in the area. Educational facilities were lacking, and there was little opportunity for employment outside of agriculture. The residents hunted, fished and tried to make a living from their land. Farmers still looked for pines to slash for "dip," but most of the longleaf pines near Bucksville were used up or had been cut for lumber. Even though the farmers and lumbermen of Horry County had contributed to the early wasteful cutting of virgin and old-growth pines, oaks and bald cypress trees along the Waccamaw, Pee Dee and Black Rivers, there were still hundreds of thousands of acres of old-growth forests remaining in the Lowcountry of South Carolina in 1885.

Rivers continued to be the main arteries of transportation and commerce well into the twentieth century. By the end of the last decade of the nineteenth century, the U.S. Corps of Engineers had removed snags and deepened portions of the Waccamaw River all the way from Georgetown to Conway. Steamboats operating out of Conway provided a regular service all along the Waccamaw, stopping at landings at Toddville, Bucksville, Bucksport, Waverly, Hagley and all of the plantation landings between Conway and Georgetown. The U.S. Corps of Engineers also deepened the channels of the Pee Dee, Santee, Congaree and Wateree Rivers, and regular steamboat routes were established between Georgetown and Charleston and from there to as far away as Columbia and Camden.

As lumber and naval stores businesses picked up in Georgetown, stores like that of J.B. Steele Grocery and Drygoods Company sprang up along Georgetown's waterfront, selling retail goods to customers along the Waccamaw, Pee Dee, Black and Santee Rivers. Steele would order wholesale goods from an agent in New York by telegraph. The agent would purchase goods from various manufacturers and suppliers in New York, Philadelphia, Baltimore or wherever they might be located. Steamships of the Clyde Line provided regular weekly service for freight and passengers from Georgetown

Steamboats *F.G. Burroughs* and *Ruth* loading at a Waccamaw River landing. *Courtesy of Horry County Archives Center.*

A Waccamaw Steamboat Line invoice to J.B. Steele, 1895. *Courtesy of Sid Hood and Sally Swineford.*

to Wilmington, North Carolina, to New York. The wholesale goods were shipped by a Clyde steamship to Clyde's terminal in Georgetown, only two blocks from Steele's store. When Steele received written or verbal requests from residents along the rivers for retail goods ranging from fertilizer to plows to barrels of flour, delivered to Steele by the river steamboat captains, he filled the orders, and the goods were transported by steamboat to the nearest landing or plantation. There was also some bartering, with farmers paying for goods with eggs, chickens or sweet potatoes, which Steele sold to other customers.

Steamboats also delivered cypress shingles, crossties, barrels of naval stores, tierces of rice, bales of cotton, tobacco and many other agricultural products from river landings to the Clyde terminal wharf in Georgetown, where they were transferred to a Clyde steamship and transported to New York and other destinations.

Chapter 6

1900–30

The Atlantic Coast Lumber Corporation of Georgetown, the Largest Lumber Mill East of the Mississippi River

By 1880, big eastern and midwestern lumber corporations had depleted almost all of the forests in their own parts of the country in efforts to satisfy increasing demands for lumber to build houses, factories, bridges, railroads and telegraph lines in those sections of the United States. After using up the forests of the Northeast and Midwest, the lumber barons moved into the South. They had sufficient financial backing to buy tens of thousands of acres of cheap land and stumpage from cash-poor southern farmers who had no use for the trees that grew there. Before 1900, four sizeable lumber companies from the Northeast and Midwest had established sawmills in Georgetown, South Carolina. Trees were cut and floated down the rivers in rafts to the mills, where they were processed and shipped out. During the late 1800s, the federal government appropriated funds to deepen the ship channel and protect the entrance to Winyah Bay with long stone jetties, which allowed deeper draft steamships to approach Georgetown. The wharves of the port of Georgetown were crowded with piles of lumber, crossties, poles, cypress shingles and barrels of naval stores, all being shipped by schooners and steamships to northeastern cities. Using modern logging and milling techniques, big lumber corporations began the process of clear-cutting the remainder of old-growth pine, oak and cypress trees in forests and bottomland along the Waccamaw, Pee Dee, Black and Santee Rivers. At the same time, more sawmills started up along other rivers of South Carolina, from south of the Santee River to the Savannah River and beyond.

Left: Charles Ranlett Flint, founder of the Atlantic Coast Lumber Corporation.

Below: This 1902 letterhead of the Atlantic Coast Lumber Corporation shows the layout of the mill.

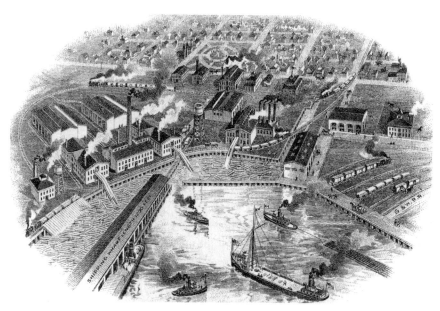

In 1900, a lumbering operation that would dwarf all of the others started up in Georgetown. The Atlantic Coast Lumber Corporation (ACL) was the brainchild of Charles Ranlett Flint, a wealthy New York City financier. Charles Flint's father, Benjamin Flint, had started life much as Henry Buck had. He had been born in 1813 in Maine, worked as a shipwright and rose through the ranks to become a ship owner and shipbuilder in Maine. He and his brother built at least one vessel per year, increasing in size each year. In 1868, they moved the shipyard from Thomaston to Bath, on the deeper Kennebec River. In 1884, the elder Flints built the famous ship *Henry B. Hyde*, 290 feet long and 2,500 tons, the largest Downeaster built in Maine up until that time. It is possible that the five-inch-thick yellow pine planks of the *Henry B. Hyde* were delivered from a Bucksville, South Carolina mill.

Benjamin Flint's son, Charles, was born in 1850 in Thomaston, Maine, and graduated from college in New York in 1868. He was an aggressive and hardworking shipping merchant and international business executive. In addition to his many other business ventures, he organized the Export Lumber Company in 1878, which grew to be one of the most successful lumber concerns in the United States, with yards in Michigan, Ottawa, Montreal, Portland, Boston and New York. In 1886, Charles, his father and his brother founded Flint and Co., a shipping and trading company located in the banking district of New York City. Charles Flint soon became known as the "Father of Trusts," handling over twenty industrial consolidations and mergers during his career, including United States Rubber Company and Computing-Tabulating-Recording Company, which became IBM.

A 1902 article in the *Kansas City Star* newspaper titled "The Very Busiest Man" describes how Charles Flint spent a typical day:

> *He goes to bed every night at 9:30 o'clock, as he cares nothing for theatres, society or art beyond the adornment of his home. At 5 o'clock in the morning, he wakes up and immediately telephones to his private secretary, who lives around the corner.*
>
> *The secretary awakens and rushes to his chief's home. As soon as he arrives there, Mr. Flint dictates letters. He dictates until breakfast is ready. The secretary eats with him as he keeps on dictating.*
>
> *Around 8:30, Mr. Flint quits dictating long enough to go out and get into his automobile. He is a skilled chauffeur.*
>
> *As he speeds down Fifth Avenue into the Wall Street section, his secretary sits behind him, notebook in hand. Often while he is dodging trucks and cars an important letter occurs to him and he dictates it on the spot.*

He is so well known to the boys of Wall Street as a chauffeur that the other day when an automobile got tangled up on Nassau Street a crowd of messengers surrounded it, hooting at the chauffeur and crying out, "You're not Charles R. Flint."

Mr. Flint and his secretary reach No. 5 Broad Street at 9 o'clock. An attendant looks after the auto, and the two at once take the elevator to the nineteenth floor. They hurry to Mr. Flint's handsome suite of rooms overlooking New York harbor.

Before he has doffed his overcoat, he has thought of several more letters, and the secretary begins taking dictation again. The morning mail takes some of his time, but while he is reading, he keeps on dictating. A room full of stenographers then emerge into his office, and the secretary begins writing out his letters. One after another, the stenographers retire after receiving their dictation.

At noon, a waiter from a nearby restaurant comes in with a menu card. Mr. Flint orders kumyss and zweibach.[10] He cares for none of the fancy dishes. While he eats his kumyss and zweibach, he dictates some more. He stops dictating when prominent businessmen come in to confer about some of the numerous business ventures with which he is connected.

Late in the afternoon, he takes his secretary in his automobile and flies away, dictating some more. Arrived at his home, he lets his secretary off for a few hours while he mounts his spirited saddle horse and takes a gallop in Central Park. After the ride, he returns to his home and spends the evening with his family.

The secretary never dares wander far from home, for at any moment he is likely to receive a hurry call to the Flint residence.

At 9:30 o'clock, Mr. Flint is wrapped in deep slumber.

Flint was also an avid sportsman, devoted to hunting, fishing and yachting. He was a member of a syndicate that built and raced the America's Cup yacht *Vigilant*. He hunted and killed big game all over the world. In 1902, he set a new world speed record with his steam-powered racing yacht *Arrow*, which was 130 feet long and 12 feet wide and equipped with two steam engines, generating four thousand horsepower. The record of forty-four miles per hour was set while roaring down the Hudson River past Grant's Tomb. Accompanying Charles Flint and the crew were his brother, Wallace, and probably his secretary, to take dictation.

---

10. Kumyss is fermented cow's milk. Zweibach is a twice-baked cracker.

Electric trams haul logs at the Atlantic Coast Lumber Corporation sawmill in Georgetown. *Courtesy of Georgetown County Digital Library.*

Tramways serve eighteen steam-dry kilns at the Atlantic Coast Lumber Corporation. Note the stacks of the mills in the background. *Courtesy of Georgetown County Digital Library.*

The four-masted schooners *City of Georgetown* and *Charles Wittmore* load lumber at the 1,200-foot wharf of the Atlantic Coast Lumber Corporation. *Courtesy of Georgetown County Digital Library.*

In 1898, when Charles Ranlett Flint organized the Atlantic Coast Lumber Corporation, he had no personal interest in the environment or the people of Lowcountry South Carolina. He knew only that many big trees grew there, that the land was cheap, that there was a port to ship lumber out as fast as possible to cities in the Northeast and that the trees in most of the rest of the country were already gone. He raised the necessary capital, hired experienced lumber executives from other parts of the country to move there, bought or leased all available timberland within one hundred miles of Georgetown and built the largest and most modern lumber mill east of the Mississippi River.

Atlantic Coast Lumber Company was a huge complex of three sawmills, stretching a half mile along the shore of the Sampit River in Georgetown. Together, these mills employed over 1,500 workers and could process over 2,500 logs per day. Before opening the mill in 1900, ACL's lawyers had obtained options on tens of thousands of acres of timberland, mostly covered with loblolly and longleaf pine, extending from the coast to more than fifty miles into the interior pine belt of South Carolina. Also, Flint had helped to successfully lobby the federal government to complete the jetties at the entrance to Winyah Bay, enabling deep-draft steamships to tie

Trio was one of several towns that sprang up along the Georgetown & Western Railroad during the lumber boom. Trio died with the demise of the lumber industry. *Courtesy of Georgetown County Digital Library.*

up at ACL's wharf. Flint formed the Atlantic Coast Steamship Company, which owned four steamships, each capable of hauling over 1 million feet of lumber per trip. They would load at ACL's 1,200-foot-long storage wharf, which could stack and store 3 million feet of lumber and could load three vessels at one time. In addition, ACL leased as many as sixteen three- and four-masted schooners, including the *City of Georgetown*, to haul lumber. After the jetties were complete and the sawmills were in full operation, the annual tonnage of lumber shipped from Georgetown jumped from 60,000 in 1900 to 300,000 in 1905.

Flint also bought and was president of the Georgetown & Western Railroad, which extended the tracks west and north, building hundreds of miles of spur tracks into the interior of South Carolina to bring logs to the Georgetown mill from forests that were too far from the rivers to transport by water. New towns sprang up along the extended lines. Where trees were close to the rivers, tugboats towed huge rafts of logs down the rivers to the mill. Wherever the cutting of timber took place, the entire tract was clear-cut, no matter whether the trees were longleaf pines, loblolly pines or hardwoods.

The inside of the mill complex was a tumultuous scene of huge machines moving violently at great speed and hurling two-ton logs about as if they were straw. Saws shrieked piercingly amid a deafening rumble of moving belts, chains and pulleys. The plant consisted of a large enclosed pond along the river, where logs were stored until they were conveyed to the upper floor of one of the three sawmills, which had multiple bandsaws, feeders, edgers, slashers and trimmers. There were eighteen steam-drying kilns with a total capacity of 500,000 feet per day, a planing mill, a ripping mill, a turpentine still, a two-thousand-gallon-per-day alcohol plant operated by DuPont and used to make gunpowder from sawdust, a shingle mill, a lath plant, complete machine shops, a foundry, a pattern shop, a car shop, a boiler shop, a blacksmith shop, a furnace and boiler house, an electrical power plant, storage warehouses, miles of electric trams, an administration building, a hotel, a commissary and housing for employees who were imported from other parts of the country.

Just as was the case in the building of the ship *Henrietta*, the managers and skilled labor for Atlantic Coast Lumber Corporation were imported from elsewhere, including northern and midwestern regions, where big lumber companies had previously operated. To entice men to live in rural South Carolina, ACL built houses and a hotel in Georgetown and at the beach resort of Pawleys Island. An ACL steamboat, the *Governor Safford*, ferried employees from Georgetown to a landing on the Waccamaw behind Pawleys Island, and an ACL train brought them from the landing to houses and a hotel along the beach. A neighborhood of homes for lower-paid employees, called Slabtown, was built in Georgetown. The houses had siding made from waste boards from the sawmill, with exposed bark on the outside.

Local men were hired for the hard labor of felling and transporting trees, for some physical labor within the mill and for the loading of ships. The grandfather and great-grandfather of Michelle Obama, wife of President Barack Obama, worked in the kilns and on the docks of Atlantic Coast Lumber Corporation for several years. Black stevedores were paid about seventy cents per day. Part of their pay was in the form of tokens that could be redeemed only at the company commissary.

Demand for lumber in the early 1900s was great, and profits from sales were high. The aim of the ACL was to cut trees, convert them into lumber and ship them to the North as quickly as possible. Between 1902 and 1906, the U.S. Bureau of Forestry sent Yale University students to South Carolina to survey the methods of various lumber companies that were engaged in lumbering in the South Carolina Lowcountry. They were impressed with the methods employed by the Burton Lumber Company, but in contrast, they discovered that the Atlantic Coast Lumber Corporation cut the forest over completely, "seemingly with no idea of ever returning again, trusting rather to their ability to buy up more land or stumpage as needed."

The differences between ACL and Henry Buck's lumber mills were not only ones of scale but also in the way profits were distributed. Buck's mills were a family business whose profits stayed largely in South Carolina. The profits of ACL went mostly out of state. The investors and executives of ACL, who were all from New York, Chicago and other faraway places, received big dividends and paychecks. Almost none of the primary investors or executives were local men. Charles Flint took no active part in the business after the first few years. He died in 1930, two years before ACL closed its doors.

Some citizens of Georgetown did profit from the increased spending by company employees and by the officers and crews of hundreds of schooners and steamships that hauled lumber from the mills. More stores and banks sprang up in Georgetown, and hopes were high that the town was growing in importance as a port. In 1905, when Georgetown celebrated its centennial of incorporation, Mayor Morgan organized large-scale parades and events, never equaled before or since. In 1906, a hurricane blew down the 160-foot ACL smokestack and damaged some mill facilities, but they were quickly repaired. In 1907, a banking crisis in New York temporarily decreased demand for lumber, and two of the ACL sawmills were shut down for a short period. In 1913, a huge fire burned two of the ACL sawmills and much of the stored lumber. The mills were replaced with a more modern concrete-and-steel sawmill. During World War I, there was a resurgence of demand for lumber, and the Atlantic Coast Lumber Corporation reached its peak of production. The U.S. government ordered the building of several hundred large wooden cargo ships, which required millions of feet of southern yellow pine. By 1918, these ships became graceful wooden ghosts, as there was no cargo and they were seldom put to sea. The lumber demands of World War I helped to finish the depletion of old-growth forests in the South.

In 1916, an article in the *American Lumberman* magazine featured the Atlantic Coast Lumber Corporation:

> *The corporation owns in fee and controls the timber rights on approximately 250,000 acres of land, bearing about 2,000,000,000 feet of lumber, board measure. The corporation owns and controls at this time enough virgin stumpage to ensure an uninterrupted cut at full mill capacity for a period of more than fifty years, with a second and even a third growth coming along on thousands of acres of land. About 75 percent of the corporation's timber is short-leaf yellow pine, 10 percent*

cypress and 15 percent other hardwoods. Being of distinctive quality, the pine has been given an individuality of its own, being sold under the name of "Atlantic Coast Soft Pine," which is practically a trademark and a guaranty of excellence.

At that time, timber was being harvested from a minimum distance of fifty miles from the mill, in the counties of Georgetown, Williamsburg, Florence, Horry, Charleston, Dorchester, Colleton and Berkeley. Logs were harvested from six scattered logging camps, each being equipped with steam-powered skidders, snakes, cableways and lifting equipment. Steam locomotives pulled as many as sixty-five log-loaded cars to the mill in one pull.

In an interview, Mr. Joseph E. McCaffrey, who worked for logging companies before the Great Depression and who retired as a vice-president of International Paper Company, described his time as a logging engineer in the South in the 1920s:

An Atlantic Coast Lumber Corporation logging crew extends a spur track through a pine forest. *Courtesy of Georgetown County Digital Library.*

An Atlantic Coast Lumber Corporation logging crew. *Courtesy of Georgetown County Digital Library.*

The men of ACL Commissary Camp Number 4 relax at noon. *Courtesy of Georgetown County Digital Library.*

In those days, there were a great many capable loggers, mostly colored, who were good skidder men, tong hookers, choker setters, levermen, loader men and riggers. White men generally didn't like to do that kind of tough work in a hot swamp and live in a log camp. Labor recruiting used to be quite a chore at times. Certain areas were known to be malaria infested and were usually avoided by loggers. In Georgia, Alabama, South Carolina, Florida and Mississippi, help-wanted ads were constantly being run in daily papers for skidding levermen, loader men, riggers, tong hookers, shop men, locomotive engineers, train crews and various types of labor required for railroad building. These crews migrated from one place to another. Most of them were nomads in some respects. Sometimes they would stay a year or two, and sometimes only a few months. In Georgetown, South Carolina, the Atlantic Coast Lumber Company at one time had the biggest mill in the United States. They cut five hundred thousand feet a day.

The 1916 article about the ACL in the *American Lumberman* was wrong about an estimated fifty-year supply of marketable timber. The pineland that was clear-cut by ACL (mostly longleaf, not short-leaf) did not regenerate quickly. What few seedlings that did regenerate grew slowly and would not reach a size suitable for marketable timber for fifty years. As early as 1909, an article appeared in the *Georgetown Semi-Weekly Times*, warning, "Yellow pine in this state is being used up rather carelessly." It went on to note, "So far as can be learned, no steps are being taken by any one of the 455 mills in this state toward replanting or otherwise securing continuity of the species. In a few years, therefore, South Carolina will be dependent on other states for her lumber supplies, as are Delaware and Utah."

During the first quarter of the twentieth century, the lumber mills of Georgetown and the surrounding areas harvested almost all of what was left of old-growth pine forests and bald cypress wetlands in the Lowcountry. The practices of clear-cutting huge tracts of land and skidding logs across the ground not only prohibited natural regeneration of the trees but also allowed destructive wildfires and removed habitat for creatures that lived in the forests. It was said that the lumber industry did more damage during those years than William Tecumseh Sherman did during his march through the South. The only device that would have allowed loggers to cut down forests any faster was the chainsaw, which although invented in the 1920s wasn't perfected as a logging tool until the 1950s. Although the people were warned that the wasteful practice of clear-cutting forests was permanently destroying the land, these large corporations continued until over 90 percent of the old-growth forests were gone. The wood in many of the big cypress logs that were cut down and made ready to be floated down the rivers to the mill was so dense that the logs sank to the bottom and were abandoned. Only recently, a few permits have been issued to allow speculators to recover old cypress sinkers, or "deadheads," from river bottoms and sell them to sawmills.

During the late 1920s, ACL realized that it was running out of trees to cut and that second-growth trees were not producing fast enough. Not surprisingly, ACL began making plans to sell its timber-depleted property as early as 1929. In 1932, the Atlantic Coast Lumber Corporation shut down its lumber operation in Georgetown and went out of business. The people of Georgetown were left without a major industry. Only a few small sawmills survived. Banks failed and downtown businesses closed as the Great Depression took hold. The people of South Carolina, who had always been dependent on products of the soil for their living, were on the verge of starvation.

Chapter 7

International Paper Company in Georgetown, the Largest Single Paper Mill in the World

International Paper Company started as a pulp and paper company in 1898, based in the northeastern United States. It expanded into Canada and the American South in the 1920s. In 1935, International Paper (IP), which had once owned substantial stock in the Atlantic Coast Lumber Corporation, made a survey of cutover pinelands in Georgetown and surrounding counties. It saw that loblolly and short-leaf pines were regenerating in cutover land where fires or livestock hadn't destroyed the seedlings. It bought much of the cutover timberland and abandoned turpentine land in Georgetown and surrounding counties that had once been owned by ACL and other lumber mills. It also bought cotton land that farmers no longer planted because of the Great Depression.

At first, IP's logging crews clear-cut the remaining pine trees on lands that it had purchased, no matter whether they were longleaf, loblolly or slash pine. There had been some natural regeneration in these tracts but not much. Soon afterward, representatives of the South Carolina Forestry Commission, the U.S. Forest Service and IP's first foresters were able to convince IP's management that the replanting of cutover land with fast-growing short-leaf pine seedlings was the first step toward obtaining a sustained yield from their forests. The new trees would be ready for initial thinning within fifteen years. Foresters also took steps to eliminate forest fires from their properties and to encourage other private landowners to grow pine trees to sell to IP. It was estimated that it would take almost one million acres of pulpwood trees to satisfy the requirements of the new Georgetown pulp and paper mill.

In 1936, International Paper started building a huge pulp and paper mill near the old ACL property. IP's Georgetown mill started operation in 1937 and, at its height, employed over 1,500 workers in the mill and another 1,000 in the forests. The new mill was a savior to the people of Georgetown. Within a few years, the mill became the largest single paper mill in the world, devouring 2,300 cords of wood per day to produce 1,800 tons of kraft paper. The mill was fed with fast-growing loblolly and short-leaf pine, which were first thinned when the stands were twelve to fifteen years old. The stands were thinned again and finally clear-cut and replanted. This thirty- to forty-year cycle was self-sustaining and was repeated over and over. Fifteen percent of the wood required by the mill was hardwood. Logs were transported to the mill by truck, train and barge and were then debarked, chipped into small pieces, cooked into pulp and made into kraft paper for paper bags and cardboard boxes. A 1948 book celebrating the fiftieth anniversary of International Paper Company stated, "Underlying all paper making is forestry. IP men are first woodmen, and increasingly today teachers and exponents of scientific tree farming. The modern paper maker is a conservationist by instinct and necessity."

For many years, IP imported some raw materials from foreign countries and exported pulp and rolls of paper to Europe and elsewhere in ships that utilized Georgetown's port. The depth of the Winyah Bay channel was increased to twenty-seven feet to accommodate larger ships. Over the years, as freighters became larger and had deeper draft, less cargo was imported and exported from Georgetown. By the 1980s, almost all raw materials and finished products of the paper mill were transported by rail or truck. Until recently, logs were cut into six-foot lengths in the forest. Many logs were transported to loading points along the rivers and the Intracoastal Waterway, where they were loaded onto big steel barges and pulled by tugboats to the mill. Eventually, IP stopped transporting logs to the mill by barge. Pine trees are now harvested in the woods in one piece, and the long logs are either delivered to the mill by truck or ground into chips at remote locations and trucked to the mill.

While working in the mill's engineering department during the summer of 1956, I observed how kraft paper was made from pulp at that time. Running twenty-four hours a day, seven days a week, the mill refined and washed tons of pulp, which were batches of cooked wood fibers from the chips of thousands of trees. The pulp was pumped to a huge building containing two side-by-side mammoth paper machines. At one end of each roaring machine, pulp was spread onto a seventeen-foot-wide, fast-moving wet screen, where it was flattened and guided between and around a series of almost one hundred horizontal, whirling, steaming cylinders called dryers, each almost ten feet in diameter, stretching one thousand feet toward the other end of the building. These cylinders squeezed the pulp into the thickness of paper and sucked out the water. Steam rose in a hot, hazy cloud from the paper machines and was blown away by giant fans. At the far end of the building, the flattened sheets were wound into a giant roll of brown paper, weighing about ten thousand pounds. The experience of standing between the two roaring, shrieking machines, which were louder than any rock concert of today, was exhilarating and even a little frightening. The wet concrete floor shook, and workers ran back and forth giving each other hand signals. A siren went off, and there was a break in the sheet of paper. A man with a paper cutter ran between two dryers, pulling piles of paper out of the way, dragging them to a hole in the floor and stuffing them into the hydropulper to be recycled. The machines seldom stopped.

During the Georgetown Kraft Mill's many years of operation, International Paper made changes and improvements. A box plant was built to manufacture cardboard boxes. A bleach plant was built that initially made stock for IBM cards and later made other bleached paper products. The Georgetown mill was the first of IP's mills to use computerized information and process control systems. Finished products changed over the years with changes in technology and market demands.

In 2006, International Paper Company, the largest private landholder in America, decided to sell most of the timberland it owned. Owners of forestland would supply the needs of IP's pulp and paper mills. Pulpwood trees would be sold to IP through timber management organizations, which negotiated with owners of forestland for trees to be cut on specific tracts. In addition to growing and selling pulpwood, most owners of pine forests allow some trees to reach pole or lumber size before they are sold. They also leave some trees for natural regeneration.

IP owned 628,000 acres in South Carolina. Between 2006 and 2011, IP sold almost all of its South Carolina forestland. The South Carolina Department of Natural Resources bought two tracts of pine forest in Lowcountry South Carolina from IP, totaling 29,000 acres, which will be protected from development. Many of the remaining tracts were sold to timber investment organizations, which were still in the process of identifying which tracts they wished to retain and which ones were going to be sold. The future of these traditional industrial forests was still very uncertain.

Everyone who lives near or passes through Georgetown, South Carolina, quickly learns something about pine trees. Parades of loaded logging trucks rumble toward that tall monster of pipes, smokestacks and steel tanks that is International Paper's Georgetown Kraft Mill. Mountains of piled pine tree trunks and wood chips feed into the mill's mouth, and out the other end comes "the smell of money," drifting with the wind across the countryside. Until the 1970s, citizens of Georgetown paid little attention to the smells and white particles that billowed out of the smokestacks at IP. They said it "smelled like money" and employees drove "mill cars" to work, whose paint jobs were already too rusty to be damaged further by emissions from the stacks. IP installed a free carwash in the mill parking lot, which both employees and other citizens of Georgetown used. During the 1990s, when pressure was put on IP to clean up its discharge of particles from its stacks and chemicals from its wastewater, the company made improvements in the quality of air and water. International Paper has been a good neighbor and the principal employer of Georgetown's citizens for over seventy-five years.

Chapter 8

Forest Restoration and Conservation in Lowcountry South Carolina

As early as 1922, the subject of forest conservation surfaced on the floor of the South Carolina House of Representatives. It was proposed that the foremost authority in the United States about forest conservation, Gifford Pinchot, who was the first chief of the U.S. Bureau of Forestry, be invited to speak to the House about reforestation. However, because he was a Republican and a Yankee, the proposal was voted down. In 1924, the next chief of the U.S. Bureau of Forestry, William Greeley, was invited to speak to the South Carolina legislature. Greeley proclaimed, "The end of the great pineries of the South is near. But there is no reason to regret having utilized our forests as we have. Any vigorous and energetic race would have done the same. But we need to begin reforestation."

The legislature gave Greeley, a hero of World War I, a standing ovation, but it took no action about reforestation. Finally, in 1927, the South Carolina Forestry Commission was established to promote the idea of sustained yields from loblolly and short-leaf pine forests, to be brought about by eliminating forest fires and by leaving some trees in cutover land to regenerate the forests. The South Carolina Forestry Commission also began to instruct landowners on the subjects of reforestation, control of wildfires and improvement of forestry management. For many years, farmers had been using fires to clear land for fields and cattle pastures without regard for damage to forests.

By 1930, at the start of the Great Depression, big lumber corporations had chewed up the forests of the South and spat them out again in the form of millions of miles of lumber. They then moved on to the forests of the Pacific coast, leaving in their wake, as historian Henry Clepper said, "hundreds of thousands of acres, cutover and burned over, that nobody wanted at any price. The little sawmill towns disintegrated among the charred stumps."

The election of Franklin Roosevelt in 1932 brought relief to some in South Carolina in the form of the National Recovery Act (NRA) and the Civilian Conservation Corps (CCC). Over three thousand members of the CCC in South Carolina planted millions of pine seedlings, erected fire towers and plowed firebreaks. Beginning in 1936, the federal government, under the auspices of the U.S. Bureau of Forestry and the South Carolina Forestry Commission, was able to buy several thousand acres of cutover timberland from lumber companies and individuals and establish the Francis Marion National Forest. The forest is located between Georgetown and Charleston and currently encompasses 260,000 acres. The primary aim of the original purchase was to provide work for South Carolina CCC workers. That purpose was accomplished, but the CCC was of little help to the other nine thousand residents who were living in or immediately around the forest in 1936. They struggled to support themselves through subsistence farming, woodwork, moonshining or a combination of all three.

The Francis Marion National Forest and several other state forests have been valuable resources for the restoration of lower South Carolina's pine forests. In addition to the twenty-eight-thousand-acre Manchester State Forest, acquired in the 1930s, the South Carolina Forestry Commission acquired the twelve-thousand-acre Wee Tee State Forest along the Santee River in 2004. Partly because of the establishment of state and national forests, loblolly and short-leaf pine and some species of hardwoods are making a comeback in lower South Carolina.

In 1939, the federal government authorized construction of a dam across the Santee and Cooper Rivers, to be owned by the South Carolina Public Service Authority, whose stated purpose was to provide electricity to residents of rural South Carolina. The hydroelectric generating station and dam-lake project were part of the NRA and employed over twelve thousand workers. It was the largest land-clearing project in the United States at that time. However, the wasteful clearing of 177,000 acres of swamps and forestland in less than three years produced 200 million board feet of lumber at a time when markets for lumber were depressed. The dam created Lake Moultrie and Lake Marion, the largest lakes in South Carolina. It diverted flow from the upper Santee River and its tributaries into the Cooper River, which empties into Charleston Harbor.

The idea of providing commercial transportation from upper South Carolina to Charleston had been popular ever since 1800, when the Santee

Canal, the first summit canal[11] in America, was built, joining the Santee River with the Cooper River. The early canal was not a financial success for a number of reasons, including lack of water during dry seasons, and was abandoned in 1850. In 1821, Robert Mills, architect for the Washington Monument and, at that time, an engineer on the South Carolina Board of Public Works, published a lengthy pamphlet describing his fanciful dream of connecting the waterways of South Carolina to the Ohio River and the Great Lakes, making Charleston competitive with all other ports in America. The 1940 Santee Cooper dam and its huge lock were built partly to promote ship traffic between Charleston and Columbia, but there was actually very little commercial traffic through the shallow lakes. Also, silt from the Santee River settled in Charleston Harbor and necessitated more frequent and costly dredging. In 1985, to rectify the dredging situation, another canal and dam were built to divert water from the Santee River back into its original estuary, located a few miles south of Winyah Bay. The two lakes have proved to be excellent facilities for tourism and recreational fishing. During construction of the original dam, many striped bass, which swam upriver to spawn, were trapped above the dam and became landlocked. They were able to survive and multiply in the lakes and rivers above the dam. South Carolina later named the striped bass as the state game fish. In 1941, the U.S. Fish and Wildlife Service established the fifteen-thousand-acre Santee National Wildlife Refuge near the recently flooded Lake Marion.

South Carolina is approximately 20.5 million acres in size, with 19.2 million acres of land and 1.3 million acres of water. In 2008, it was estimated that 12.9 million acres of land in South Carolina were forested. The forest-products industry is the number-one manufacturing industry in the state and employs over ninety thousand people. With an ever-increasing statewide population, South Carolina is seeing a tremendous rise in residential and commercial development, and many of South Carolina's forestlands are being converted to non-forest uses.

The South Carolina chapter of the Nature Conservancy, the South Carolina Conservation Bank, the South Carolina Coastal Conservation League, the Pee Dee Land Trust, the Lowcountry Open Land Trust, the Audubon Society, the Congaree Land Trust, the Winyah Bay Focus Group, the ACE Basin Task Force, the South Carolina Department of Natural Resources, the Sierra Club, Ducks Unlimited and several other conservation

---

11. A summit canal is one in which vessels are raised from a body of water by a series of locks to a canal at a higher elevation and at the other end of that canal the vessels are lowered by a series of locks into another body of water.

organizations have encouraged landowners to enter into conservation easement agreements, which perpetually protect their land from being developed or logged in environmentally unfriendly ways. Through additional efforts of these conservation organizations, some wealthy landowners who had bought old rice plantations for duck-hunting preserves and other purposes after the Civil War, including the Huntingtons, Baruchs, Yawkeys, Duponts, Donnelleys, the Santee Gun Club and others, have donated large tracts of land to the state or federal government to become wildlife preserves or protected forests. Recently, some of the protected wetlands that were once impounded to become rice fields have reverted to their original state and are supporting the growth of bald cypress trees. During the late twentieth century, longleaf pine, bald cypress and hardwood forests in some parts of Lowcountry South Carolina began to make a comeback.

There are several abandoned rice plantations included in the nine-thousand-acre tract along the Waccamaw River, south of Henry Buck's properties, that Archer and Anna Huntington purchased in 1930. The property, today known as Brookgreen Gardens, contains the largest museum of outdoor sculpture in the United States and was begun by sculptor Anna Hyatt Huntington. The property has been donated by the Huntington family to a private foundation, which manages and protects it. The tract contains almost one thousand acres of old-growth longleaf pine forest.

The Nature Conservancy has acquired several tracts of land to ensure their long-term protection. Sandy Island is a sixteen-thousand-acre island bounded by the Waccamaw River, the Pee Dee River and Bull Creek south of what used to be Henry Buck's Tip Top Plantation. It is the largest freshwater island along the eastern seaboard. In 1993, two wealthy businessmen owned the entire island except for about two hundred acres, which were owned by about two hundred black descendants of Henry Buck's and other planters' slaves, who had lived there since the Civil War. The businessmen applied to the State Department of Transportation for a permit to build a bridge from Tip Top to the island so that they could cut the bald cypress and longleaf pine trees on the island and transport them to a mainland lumber mill. Sensing that the building of a bridge would eventually lead to development of the island as a huge residential community for retirees, the Nature Conservancy and the South Carolina Coastal Conservation League acted to have the bridge permit denied. The Nature Conservancy then entered into negotiation to buy the property, and with the help of the state, it was able to purchase nine thousand acres and place valuable forests under permanent protection.

As another example, in 2012, the Nature Conservancy purchased 2,100 acres in Carvers Bay, in part to protect the habitat of the black bear population. Deanna Ruth, a biologist with the South Carolina Department of Natural Resources, is well acquainted with the Carvers Bay black bears that take advantage of the impenetrable jungle of bay vegetation to den and raise their young. Ruth notes, "Carvers Bay provides our coastal bears with excellent habitat that fits into a larger corridor of undeveloped land along the Pee Dee and Little Pee Dee Rivers."

The South Carolina Department of Natural Resources (SCDNR) also owns the 5,300-acre Waccamaw River Heritage Trust area, a bottomland hardwood forest along the Waccamaw River just north of Conway. It is also black bear habitat. In addition, SCDNR manages 1,600 acres of wetlands and forest along the lower Waccamaw River, donated by Thomas G. Samworth.

SCDNR owns or manages many other properties throughout the state, including the 24,000-acre Santee Coastal Reserve Wildlife Management Area, which includes most of the Santee River Delta and adjacent islands. The largest and one of the most important coastal properties managed by SCDNR is the 140,000-acre ACE Basin, located between Charleston and Beaufort. The ACE Basin, named for the Ashepoo, Combahee and Edisto Rivers, was designated as a National Estuarine Research Reserve by NOAA in 1992 and is the third-largest reserve in the nation.

A second National Estuarine Research Reserve is located along the northern border of Winyah Bay and extends northward to include North Inlet, an ocean-dominated unpolluted estuary. The twelve-thousand-acre reserve is part of Hobcaw Barony, a tract of protected land on Waccamaw Neck. Hobcaw Barony is overseen by the Baruch Foundation and consists of wetlands, former rice fields, upland hardwood and pine forests and barrier islands.

SCDNR was able to buy or lease 71,000 acres of forest across the state because of the Forest Legacy Program, passed by the U.S. Congress in 1990. The program's purpose is to identify and protect environmentally important forestlands that are threatened with conversion to non-forest uses. Because South Carolina's Lowcountry has become such a popular vacation and retirement area, the amount of land being converted from forest to residential development has increased rapidly. In 2006, SCDNR, assisted by the Forest Legacy Program and the Nature Conservancy, purchased the 25,668-acre Woodbury Tract in Marion County and the 13,281-acre Hamilton Ridge Tract in Hampton County from International Paper Company, utilizing Heritage Trust revenue bonds issued by the State of South Carolina. More recently, a lack of federal and state funding has limited acquisition of additional forestland.

In 1932, the U.S. Fish and Wildlife Service bought sixty-six thousand acres and established the Cape Romain National Wildlife Refuge. The Cape Romain Refuge extends for twenty-two miles along the beaches of barrier islands between Georgetown and Charleston. The refuge includes Bull Island, which was one of the first sources of live oak used for shipbuilding in America. According to Virginia Wood, in her book, *Live Oaking*:

> *In 1799, the United States government entered into a contract with Thomas Shubrick of Bulls Island to provide live oak for the frames of 74-gun ships of the line for the US Navy. With forty black carpenters and sixty shipwrights from Massachusetts, five of whom died on the job, he was unable to complete on schedule even one frame of a 74-gun vessel because of "the immense labor required." So much of the live oak timber on Bulls Island was rotten that he could eventually supply only two-thirds of one ship's frames.*

Most of the rest of the required live oak was obtained in Georgia and Florida. More recently, live oak timbers from trees that were cut down to expand a highway in Charleston were used in the 1995 restoration of the USS *Constitution*.

In 1997, the U.S. Fish and Wildlife Service established the 54,000-acre Waccamaw National Wildlife Refuge south of Conway. At one time, Henry Buck owned some of that land. By 2007, 10,590 acres had been purchased and another 27,000 acres were under long-term lease. The area includes many types of habitat, including flooded alluvial bottomlands, upland longleaf pine forests and remnant plantation tidal rice fields.

Francis Beidler and Harry Hampton are two individuals who contributed much to the preservation of South Carolina's bottomland forests. Francis Beidler was a Chicago lumber tycoon who, by 1900, had acquired hundreds of thousands of acres of South Carolina bottomland swamps that drained into the Congaree, Wateree, Santee or Edisto Rivers. He found it extremely difficult to log these remote swamps and by 1915 had abandoned his efforts to cut and remove bald cypress and tupelo trees, some over one thousand years old. He placed the old-growth forests in reserve. In 1969, the Nature Conservancy and the Audubon Society purchased fifteen thousand acres from the Beidler family within Four Holes Swamp, located along the Edisto River northwest of Charleston, which included the world's largest virgin cypress-tupelo swamp forest. It was named the Francis Beidler Forest.

Old-growth bottomland cypress trees, Congaree National Park. *Photo by Mary McAlister.*

In 1976, with ongoing help from South Carolina conservationist and writer Harry Hampton, a 27,000-acre parcel of the Congaree River swamp, part of the Cowasee Basin, located along the Congaree River south of Columbia, was acquired by the federal government from the Beidler family's heirs. In 2003, it was designated Congaree National Park. The 215,000-acre Cowasee Basin is bounded by the Congaree, Wateree and Santee Rivers. Congaree National Park is South Carolina's only national park and contains the last stand of old-growth bottomland hardwood forest in the southeastern United States. There are many very large bald cypress and tupelo trees, as well as six national champion trees: a 160-foot-tall loblolly pine, a sweetgum, a laurel oak, a water hickory, a deciduous holly and a swamp tupelo. This magnificent park stands as an example of how other bottomland swamps of Lowcountry South Carolina would look today if the trees hadn't been destroyed by logging or development.

Because of their long growing cycle, it has taken a long time for foresters to persuade landowners to replant longleaf pine forests. In good soil, longleaf pines can reach a size suitable for pole timber in about thirty years. Saw timber sizes take much longer, and not many landowners want to think that far ahead. Only in recent years have some landowners been convinced by forest managers to plant forests of longleaf pine. It was finally realized that

Old-growth pine trees, Congaree National Park. *Photo by Mary McAlister.*

by eliminating the grazing of livestock in longleaf pine forests, by allowing periodic controlled fires in the forests and by careful forestry management, the regeneration of longleaf forests could be successful. While the trees are maturing, straw from longleaf pine needles can be sold as mulch. Foresters are hopeful that South Carolina will regenerate more of its longleaf forests, which long ago were part of the largest longleaf pine forest in America.

Despite the efforts of conservation groups to protect forests from misuse, there are still threats to the forests of South Carolina and the rest of the South. As an example, in February 2013, a giant Austrian lumber operator, Klausner Holding USA, proposed to build a 700-million-board-foot-per-year mega lumber mill in South Carolina. The proposed mill would be one of if not the largest mill in the world. The mill would dwarf all other mills, possibly put them out of business and probably again devastate the pine forests of South Carolina. One existing mill owner darkly joked that Klausner's effect on forests could eventually give Orangeburg, South Carolina, a clear view of the Atlantic Ocean even though it is some seventy-five miles away. Politicians, landowners, developers and conservationists argued about short-term gains versus long-term effects of such a mill, and the outcome has not yet been determined.

Another recent dilemma for pine forest owners in the South was the small difference in selling price between pulpwood and saw timber, which discouraged owners from waiting for trees to grow to saw timber size. This also led to a drop-off in the planting of seedlings for trees that were meant to become saw timber. Other threats to forests are a result of climate change, including forest destruction by wildfires during times of drought and by high winds during hurricanes. In 1989, Hurricane Hugo snapped off thousands of pine trees in the Francis Marion National Forest and destroyed most of the nesting habitat for the largest population of the endangered red-cockaded woodpecker in America.

A further challenge for conservationists has been trying to control the quality of water and the amount of silt in the rivers that flow through Winyah Bay and into the Atlantic Ocean. The eighteen-thousand-square-mile watershed of the Pee Dee, Waccamaw, Black, Santee and Sampit Rivers and their tributaries is the third-largest watershed in the eastern United States. The Pee Dee River furnishes by far the greatest quantity of water flowing into Winyah Bay. In North Carolina, the name of the Pee Dee River changes to the Yadkin River. The alluvial Yadkin River and its tributaries flow past several fast-growing urban areas, including Winston-Salem, Greensboro and Salisbury, where runoffs from developed land increase sedimentation and erosion of the banks of streams and rivers. Farther downstream are a series of eighteen dams and recreational lakes, decreasing flow downstream. Several municipal water systems take water from the river. Treated and untreated industrial and agricultural waste is dumped into the river. Below the last dam of the Yadkin River, near the North Carolina–South Carolina border, the Pee Dee River's banks are eroded by runoff from agricultural fields and from some pulpwood tracts and skid trails in forests that have been clear-cut but not yet reforested. Farther downstream, a canal draws water from the Pee Dee River and delivers it to the International Paper Company mill in Georgetown and to the Georgetown municipal water system. Where the Pee Dee River joins the Waccamaw River and the Intracoastal Waterway, near Myrtle Beach, runoff and waste from Myrtle Beach resorts are added to the river. Farther downstream, sediment from fields along the Black River is added. Where the Pee Dee passes through Georgetown and becomes Winyah Bay, sediment from the tidal Sampit River and wastewater from Georgetown's industries and the city of Georgetown flow into Winyah Bay. The Santee River flows down from above Charlotte, North Carolina, and Columbia and Camden, South Carolina, until it reaches the Santee Cooper diversion dam. Below the dam, most of the Lower Santee River flows through its own estuary into the Atlantic Ocean. However, some water from the Lower Santee flows through the Estherville-Minim Canal and into Winyah Bay, depositing more silt. In addition, a five- to six-foot tide flows in and out of Winyah Bay from the Atlantic Ocean, depositing sand from the ocean onto the bottom of the bay.

In the nineteenth century, before jetties, dams, pollution, erosion and sedimentation changed Winyah Bay, shellfish, saltwater and freshwater fish of all kinds, land birds, waterfowl, wading birds, shorebirds and all creatures of the salt marshes lived in profusion in or along the wooded shores of the bay. Sturgeon, shad, striped bass and other species of fish swam through the bay and up the rivers to spawn. As late as the middle of the twentieth century, there were commercial fish houses, caviar processors, an oyster factory, a shrimp-processing plant and a menhaden factory in or near Georgetown. The numbers and species of fish and other wildlife in the bay declined during the second half of the twentieth century, partly because of development and pollution.

At the beginning of the twentieth century, the Winyah Bay ship channel was dredged to a depth of eighteen feet and later to twenty-seven feet. At first, spoil from dredging was deposited in the marshes alongside the channel. As the depth of the channel was increased, it shoaled more quickly, requiring more frequent dredging. As runoff into the rivers above Georgetown from industrial plants and developed land increased, Winyah Bay became more polluted. Recently, regulations have been put into place and enforced to reduce but not entirely eliminate pollution and runoff into the rivers that flow into the bay. Fish and wildlife have made somewhat of a comeback, although Winyah Bay will never be as healthy as it was two hundred years ago. There is less fresh water flowing into the bay than before the dams were built, and ocean water temperatures and levels are rising, both of which affect wildlife in Winyah Bay and its rivers. Also, brackish water intrudes farther up the rivers during droughts, which have become more common in recent years.

The current health of the rivers feeding into Winyah Bay varies greatly. No longer are schooners being towed up the rivers by steam tugs to load lumber, nor are rafts of logs being floated downriver to lumber mills. No longer do steamboats bring rice and naval stores to Georgetown and take supplies upriver to landings and plantations. None of the rivers are being used for commerce, and most of them are navigable for small boats only because of bridges, dams or shallow depths of water. Even the Intracoastal Waterway has little commercial traffic. Today, the rivers are most valued for fishing, exploring and enjoying the beauty of the undeveloped portions of their shorelines.

Since 2009, American Rivers, Waccamaw Riverkeeper of Winyah Rivers Foundation and Pee Dee Land Trust have been working in conjunction with other conservation stakeholders to establish the Waccamaw River Blue Trail. This effort, funded by the Gaylord and Dorothy Donnelley Foundation, is using recreation as a tool to promote land conservation within the Waccamaw watershed. These efforts are ongoing and have been rewarded by recognition of the Waccamaw River Blue Trail as a priority project of the America's Great Outdoors Initiative and the selection of the South Carolina portion of the Blue Trail as a National Water Trail.

Additionally, conservation organizations are successfully promoting the idea of landowners selling conservation easements for forestlands in danger of destruction or development. These easements allow forests to be managed in such a way that trees grow to mature size, provide habitat for native birds and animals and, once again, allow rural South Carolina to become as beautiful as it once was. A continuous cycle of planting, cutting and replanting fast-growing species of pine trees has proven to be economically successful to supply wood for our industrial needs. Struggles continue between developers, who want to remove forests in order to provide residential and commercial space for South Carolina's increasing population, and conservationists, who want to maintain the beauty of nature and preserve resources for public use.

Despite the conservation and reforestation successes enumerated above, Lowcountry South Carolina faces major ecological problems caused by rapid recent and expected increases in population throughout our region. Retirees and tourists flock toward views of the ocean and rivers. Developers pay owners of sensitive forest and bottomland tracts higher prices than conservation organizations can pay to protect land from development. As residential and commercial development increases, forest acreage is decreased and runoff and pollution of rivers is increased. The pleasures of living and enjoying nature in Lowcountry South Carolina are being destroyed by the increasing numbers of commercial developments along the beaches and rivers.

Other major environmental problems result from changes in climate. Increasingly frequent storms cause oceanfront destruction, flooding of rivers and wind damage in forests. Increasingly frequent droughts cause water shortages in rivers and wildfires in forests. Rising sea levels and temperatures cause saltwater intrusion in rivers and adverse effects to coastal wildlife. As sea levels rise, beach erosion is made worse, in part by past decisions to construct jetties, groins and sea walls along the coast, prohibiting the natural migration of barrier islands.

The rivers, beaches and forests of coastal South Carolina are still among the most beautiful in America. However, if their unique beauty is to remain and be preserved for future generations, the landowners and influential citizens of Lowcountry South Carolina will have to place more value on the quality of the environment than on their desire to gain wealth. They and other South Carolinians must act to protect the beauty and public access to the forests and rivers of Lowcountry South Carolina.

Epilogue
A Summer in the Swamps

The swamps of Lowcountry South Carolina are inspiring and beautiful in winter, spring and fall, but summer can be another story. As an example, in June 1777, the nineteen-year-old Marquis Gilbert de Lafayette, the famous French "Boy General" of the American Revolution, arrived inside of the entrance to Winyah Bay from France in the ship *Victoire* after fifty-four days at sea. Rowing toward the shore of North Island at night in their jolly boat, Lafayette, Baron De Kalb and some of the ship's crew grounded in the mud on a falling tide. They were forced to slosh through the marsh muck, finally arriving at the summer home of a rice planter, who put them up for the night—Lafayette's first night in America. The next day, Lafayette decided to go on horseback and on foot to Charlestown to avoid the possibility of being captured at sea by the English. Lafayette, De Kalb and several others set out on horseback through the swamps toward Charlestown and finally arrived there three days later "in wretched condition." According to one of Lafayette's officers, "We arrived looking like beggars and brigands. People mocked us when we said we were French officers here to defend their liberty."

Lafayette had lived through a new experience, a summer trek through the swamps and trackless woods of Lowcountry South Carolina.

My own summer swamp experience began in Georgetown in June 1954. Each year, International Paper Company hired a few college students for summer work. As a nineteen-year-old college sophomore, I was assigned to the Bull Gang, cutting brush outside of the paper mill fence. On the second day of work, an office employee appeared and asked if there were any engineering students who would like to volunteer to be laborers on a survey crew. Two of us volunteered and were told to report to the woodyard shack the next day at 7:30 a.m.

The next morning, Phil and I found our way to the woodyard shack, which stood between mountains of stacked logs. There was a pleasant smell of sap from the log piles, and flocks of swallows swooped down and around the piles. Outside of the shack was the deafening sound of tumbling logs in the debarking drums and the shriek of a log chipper as it turned big logs into little chips in one second. We met the IP wood yard foreman, Mr. Louis Overton, an old gentleman who said he had once been an officer of the Atlantic Coast Lumber Corporation. We also met Jake, who was to be the crew chief, our boss. He was accompanied by a tall, distinguished elderly man with thick eyeglasses who was introduced as Mr. Pollard, chief engineer for B.P. Barber Engineers, which had a contract with IP to design and survey a new canal to bring fresh water to the mill from the Pee Dee River. Mr. Pollard explained that the mill required large amounts of fresh water to clean the pulp before it was made into paper and to generate steam to cook the wood chips. Ever since the mill started in 1937, IP had been getting water from a pump station along the nearby Black River, which had been taken over from the Atlantic Coast Lumber Corporation. However, current demands for water for the mill were much greater, and during recent summer droughts, the Black River water was being contaminated by salt water backing up from Winyah Bay at high tide. A new source of fresh water was needed, and IP had decided to build a canal to the mill from a new pump station, twenty-five miles up the Pee Dee River. Our survey crew was to cut and mark a centerline for that canal.

Outside of the shack, we were joined by three black men, veteran IP laborers at the paper mill. Kenny, Frank and Pinckney piled into the back of Jake's pickup truck alongside Phil and me. Mr. Pollard rode in the front with Jake. We were driven to a truck trailer, where tools were stored. Each of us was given a double-edged bush axe. Jake ordered us to put two heavy axes and three machetes in the back of the truck, along with sharpening files, a sledgehammer, a bundle of wooden stakes, a first-aid kit and a snakebite kit. He then stowed his survey equipment—two range poles, a level rod, a one-hundred-foot steel measuring chain and some steel stakes—all crammed into the back of the pickup. He placed his pride and joy, a wooden box with his West German transit in it, plus a tripod, in the front seat next to Mr. Pollard. We sat on the sides of the back of the pickup as Jake drove out of

Georgetown, headed west. He stopped in a field a couple of miles out of town. Mr. Pollard looked at the five of us in the back of the truck, smiled and said, "Gentlemen, this is where we begin." Kenny, Frank and Pinckney said, "Yassuh," climbed out of the truck and prepared for whatever was next. Phil and I gave a blank look and waited for orders.

Mr. Pollard rolled out a set of blueprints on the hood of the pickup. Jake set his tripod over a stake that Mr. Pollard had stuck in the ground. Jake then set the transit box on the ground, carefully opened it and lifted the instrument (which he assured us was worth thousands of dollars) out of the box, screwed it onto the tripod and leveled it up. He pointed the telescope in the magnetic direction that Mr. Pollard ordered and told me to take one end of the one-hundred-foot chain and a range pole and walk out in the direction that the telescope pointed. Phil held the other end of the chain below a plumb bob that dangled from the center of the tripod. When I reached the end of the chain, I held the range pole straight up and down, and Jake directed me to move it right and left until the eight-foot red-and-white-striped pole was lined up with the crosshairs of the transit telescope. Kenny brought a wood stake and the sledge. He drove it flush with the ground. We pulled the chain tight, put a tack in the center of the top of the stake and drove in a marker stake with a red ribbon next to it. Jake lettered the station number on the marker stake with a blue keel.

We didn't know it at the time, but we would repeat that operation one thousand times before the summer was over. The first few stations were easy, crossing open fields or cutting brush with machetes. We passed through a stand of small pine trees that first day, clearing out an eight-foot-wide path along the canal centerline. Kenny, Frank and Pinckney did most of the cutting, but we were all hot and tired by 4:30 p.m., when we knocked off for the day. We had progressed almost a mile. Jake drove us back to the woodyard shack, where we stowed our tools. Mr. Pollard told us how fortunate we were to be part of the crew that would make history by crossing twenty-five miles of ground that no one had crossed since the time of Columbus. He said he wished he could stay with us but that he had to return to Columbia. He told us goodbye and said he would be back in a week or two.

Phil lived in Georgetown, so I told him I would see him tomorrow. I drove north on Highway 17 to Pawleys Island, where I had rented a room in the back of the only drugstore on the island, leased for the summer by two college friends of mine. I stripped the sweaty clothes from my itchy body and took a shower, at which point I discovered I had been invaded by dozens of burrowing ticks. I picked off fifty-seven of the disgusting creatures, praying

I had found them all. The itching was still there, caused by chiggers that had dropped from pine trees, crawled onto my bare skin, spit and jumped to the ground, leaving red welts. I had a feeling this was going to be a long, hot summer.

The next day, Phil advised me to wear a cap, boots and long-sleeved shirt and to rub turpentine on my clothes. He suggested dousing myself with citronella for mosquitoes and rubbing sulfur on my clothes to ward off deer flies. He was a local boy who had been around the woods all of his life, and I soon learned to take all of his advice. Phil and I were taken aside by Jake, who was a big jolly redheaded man of about forty-five. We soon found out he liked to brag about his athletic accomplishments and tell tall tales. He had a twinkle in his eye when he told a story that everybody knew was a lie. He knew what he was doing, though, when it came to using his survey instrument. He kept it in spotless condition and dared anyone to touch it when he had it set up and ready for a shot down the line. He liked to kid Phil and me about being engineering students. "You think you're engineers? Ha! You ain't nothin but pimples on an engineer's ass." And he'd spit another squirt of tobacco juice toward Phil's shoes. Kenny, Frank and Pinckney would just chuckle and get back to work.

By the end of the first week, we had cut our way through two loblolly pine forests and were in the middle of our first swamp. We had to hold on to limbs and vines to avoid slipping and tripping on the slippery roots and knees of cypress trees, hidden by green scum. Thorny vines were like razor wire that you had to cut away with machetes or a bush axe. There must have been a thousand mosquitoes. Kenny Kinlock killed the first water moccasin, which was followed by many others. During that summer, we killed every kind of poisonous snake in North America except a coral snake, and we killed three kinds of rattlesnakes, one with seventeen rattles. The ones that got away were the ones that scared you.

Each day, we would try to find some decent place in the shade to eat the lunches we had brought, usually packs of Nabs, Moon Pies and a Mountain Dew or an RC Cola. Jake brought a big thermos of lemonade laced with salt, which he would share at times of the day when it was so hot you thought the monkey was on your back. During lunchtime, we would talk about anything that came into our minds. Kenny, the most senior man, talked about being a soldier in Europe during World War II. "I was a Truman soldier. We was hell in them days." Jake would always top anyone else's story.

One Friday, Jake was off for the day. He had begun to trust Phil to carry the transit box and had showed him how to set up the transit and level it on the tripod, so Phil was the crew chief for that day. I drove the truck to near where we had quit the day before. We were in a forest of old pines and hardwoods, nearing the Black River. Everything was going ok that day until we noticed a big pine, almost two feet in diameter, right on the centerline of the canal. It would have to be cut down. Kenny said he would do most of the cutting with the big axe if he could take the rest of the day off. Kenny said he would fell the tree off to the side, where there was a clearing. The transit was set up about fifty feet behind the tree. By the time Kenny notched it, he was sweating like a pig. He took off his shirt, exposing a nasty pink scar that ran diagonally across his black chest. As he rested, he told us about a long-ago knife fight that put him in the hospital and almost killed the other guy.

Kenny started back on the tree. The rest of us watched as big resinous chips flew out of a deep cut in the tree and the top trembled and swayed. The big pine began to lean toward the clearing, but just as we thought it was going to fall in the direction that Kenny intended, it twisted in the cut and started to fall directly toward Jake's extremely valuable survey instrument. Knowing that his job—and probably his health—were at stake, Phil took off running toward the instrument. He tackled the tripod and kept running as pine branches scraped down his back and knocked him down. He managed to keep the transit from ever touching the ground. The trunk of the tree had driven the stake where the transit had been set up deep into the ground. We laughed about it, but we knew we would have been in deep trouble if Jake's transit had been destroyed. Jake's undamaged West German beauty was back in its felt-lined box when he was ready to set it up the following Monday.

A few days later, we had reached the Black River, sighted across it and set up on the far side. The canal would cross under the Black River in big pipes when it was built. We sat on logs, sharpening the edges of our bush axes and machetes with files, preparing to cut from where we had finished the day before. We were at the top of a bluff overlooking the Black River. I walked to the edge of the bluff and started down a slope to the riverbank. Suddenly, about ten feet away were half a dozen big alligators, sunning or sleeping on the muddy riverbank. About that time, they saw me and started scrabbling toward the river. The big, ugly creatures, about ten or twelve feet long, were awkward but quick as they thrashed their tails, glided toward the middle of the river and sank out of sight. Thankfully, they seemed to have been as scared of me as I was of them.

It was a miserably hot July, and we were cutting between Black Steer Swamp and Machine Bay. Bays are large natural elliptical depressions in low flat lands that aren't connected to any creek or river. They might be full of water in the rainy season, but some are almost dry in summer. Big yellow deer flies were glad to see us because the deer had moved to wetter places and we were all they had to eat. They would fly around my head, trying to land in my ear. The only way to get rid of one was to let him land on my arm, wait until he was biting me through my shirt and then kill him with one hard swat. There was hardly any shade in the bays, just thick jumbles of cane, brush and vines, a little higher than our heads. We would take turns cutting with bush axes and machetes, making slow progress. When we knocked off for the day, we trudged back to the truck. Before returning to the mill, Jake always stopped at the Plantersville General Store to smoke a cigarette and drink a Coke. The proprietor sold all of us our Cokes but wouldn't allow Kenny, Frank and Pinckney to stay inside of the store. He made them go outside to drink. They didn't complain; they were used to Jim Crow.

It took longer and longer for Jake to find country roads or logging trails that led anywhere near where we were working. Phil was a big help because he knew all of the back roads of Georgetown County and had the best sense of direction. We started referring to him as "Boone." We had to work longer hours to get in a good day of cutting, but we didn't mind because we earned overtime pay. Sometimes it would be almost 6:00 p.m. before we were back at the mill. One morning, when we first reached the place where we would start to cut, Frank saw a big pile of shit right in the middle of the canal path that we had cut the day before. "Bear shit," Phil commented. He said he knew that bears lived in these swamps and that some people hunted them. He doubted they would bother us. That same day, Pinckney got stung by a hornet and went screaming and running around in circles until Jake got out his first-aid kit and tried to find something to put on the sting. Jake finally rubbed some tobacco juice on the sting, and Pinckney said it felt better.

The next day, we were cutting through the reeds when Phil said he smelled something off to the side of the line. The closer we got, the stronger the smell became. "It's a mash pit," said Kenny. "Somebody's makin' corn liquor." Sure enough, there was a pit dug out of the peat, and it was half full of stinking mash. It was old and had been abandoned. There was no copper still or any sign that the pit had been used recently. Late that afternoon, we were cutting through some thick woods when straight ahead of us, right on line with the center of the canal, was a copper still. Nobody was around, but there were mason jars and signs that moonshiners had been there recently. Frank and Kenny said that they didn't want to be anywhere near where moonshiners were. They were a rough bunch who didn't like black folks. Jake said he wasn't scared but that because it was Friday, we would knock off early and give the moonshiners a chance to relocate.

Sure enough, when we came back on Monday, everything was gone. We hadn't seen a soul in those woods since we started the canal until that afternoon. Phil thought he heard something a ways behind us. He thought it might be a deer. The next thing we knew, there were two scruffy white guys walking barefooted across the sharp stalks and stickers and up the rough path we had cut. They had no shirts on and looked like they needed a haircut and a shave. We stopped working and watched them approach. One of them said, "What are you all doin? This is our land, and you all better git off from it." It was hard to imagine that anyone could have lived in such a remote and inhospitable swamp.

About that time, Phil recognized the other guy. He was a man that Phil's uncle, a deputy sheriff, had arrested the year before for illegally selling fish. Phil had helped his uncle catch the man. Phil tried to hide his face behind Jake and me, but the man recognized Phil and yelled that he was going to kill him. He lunged toward Phil, but Jake grabbed the stout eight-foot range pole and drew it back. "You come one more step and I'll knock your goddamned head off. Now, both of you get the hell out of here and don't come back." They said they would leave but that they would be back the next day with a gun. They turned and walked back the way they had come. We were shaken, especially Phil. He explained the situation to Jake, and it was agreed that Phil would have to go back to the Bull Gang—at least until we were cutting farther down the line. When we returned the next day, there was no sign of them. Everything went back to normal, and we never saw them again.

By the first of August, it was hotter than hell. The temperature in the middle of the day was almost one hundred, as it had been for most of the summer. It almost never rained, and the humidity was about 100 percent. Jake said he hoped his transit wouldn't overheat and explode. We were out of the swamps and reeds and were approaching Carvers Bay, one of the most isolated places in South Carolina. "Nobody's been through here since the Indians," commented Jake. Kenny spotted a big rattler sliding into a hollow stump. We were afraid to pass by it because he might be there when we came back, so Kenny chopped on the stump until the snake slithered out, raising up and rattling like hell. Kenny cut its head off with a bush axe. It had seventeen rattles and was twelve feet long.

Phil came back on the crew about the time we started cutting in Carvers Bay. Carvers Bay is a very big swamp, covering over ten square miles. It was

"A Dream of Summer in the Swamps of South Carolina." *Etching by Charlie McAlister.*

usually wet and boggy, but 1954 had been a dry summer, and there was no water in the swamp at all. In fact, there had been a forest fire during the spring in the part of Carvers Bay where we were to start cutting. The fire had charred all of the trees, burned up the bushes and continued to burn the peat under the ground. The peat smoldered, and acrid smoke rose up like a fog. When we walked through the burned-out swamp, it was like walking on bedsprings because the peat under the roots was gone. We were supported only by the springy roots and had to be careful not to fall through the roots into a hole.

When we reached the far side of the burned part, a distance of over a mile, there were no trees, just a wall of closely packed scrubby bushes and vines about ten feet high. There was no way of walking through it or around it. The brush was so thick that only two of us at a time had room to swing a bush axe in the six-foot path that we were clearing. Two men hacked and hacked for thirty minutes until they were covered with sweat and ready to drop. Then, two other guys started cutting. When we rested, there was no place to sit in the shade. We sat in the path, drinking from Jake's thermos of salt-laced lemonade. It was too far to go back to the truck for lunch, so we stopped for thirty minutes, with the sun overhead, to eat whatever we'd brought in our paper sacks. We had to knock off almost an hour early to walk back over two miles to the truck, which was in the closest place Jake could find to park.

One day, Kenny was cutting when a big thorn from a vine broke off in the palm of his hand. It was in deep, and he couldn't pull it out. He reached in his pocket, pulled out a long switchblade knife, a pig sticker, and handed it to me. "Cut this out," he ordered, showing me the thorn. I probed gingerly into the palm of his hand, but I didn't have the guts to cut any deeper. "Shit, gimme that thing," Kenny said. He stuck it in to the base of the thorn, pulled out the thorn and sucked the blood. He picked up his bush axe and went back to cutting. About that time, two crows flew over us, cawing as they headed somewhere. Kenny looked up at the cloudless sky and said, "You know what them crows are sayin? They're sayin, 'Carva, Carva.' They know this ain't no place to be. Ha!" Jake tried to be positive about the situation. "Not far to go now, fellas. The steel tower of the World War II bombing range is supposed to be on the other side of Carvers Bay, and I think we'll see it soon." He was wrong. It was more than a few miles away.

It was about that time that I started to wonder why I had allowed myself to get into this kind of job in the first place. I began to think of some way to get out of Carvers Bay. Finally, one day, a Friday, I think, I told Jake that I wanted to cut first. I picked up my extra-sharp bush axe and began to swing with special vengeance. All of a sudden, I hit a big vine, and the double-edged axe sprang back and bit into my right forefinger. Blood squirted out. I held out my right hand as Jake looked it over. "You're going to need stitches. Kenny, you walk back with him and drive him back to the mill infirmary."

I tied a handkerchief around my hand, held it tight and walked the two miles back to the truck. Kenny turned to me with a smile and asked, "Did you do that on purpose?" "Who, me?" I smiled back. As we got in the truck, another cawing crow flew over. "I guess you won't be hearin' them Carva crows no more this summer."

When I got back to the mill infirmary, they called Dr. John Assey. He drove over, looked at the finger and told me it was too late for novocaine but that it wouldn't hurt much. He sewed it up, bandaged it and told me not to do that kind of work for the rest of the summer.

The following Monday, I was assigned to be rod man for the surveyor who was going to check the bottom elevations of the canal along the centerline that we had already cut. I reported to Mr. Gandy, a crusty old engineer in his seventies who didn't seem to care whether I was handicapped or not. He declared that I could hold the level rod with one hand as well as I could with two. We started to work our way from the mill toward the Pee Dee River, one hundred feet at a time. I rested the level rod on each stake that we had driven in the ground, and Mr. Gandy recorded the elevation in his notebook. Although I hadn't thought that I ever wanted to see that canal again, I sort of enjoyed remembering our experiences along the way. Mr. Gandy didn't seem to be in a hurry and didn't mind resting in the shade every few minutes. He was an interesting old character, telling me about all the properties he had surveyed during the past fifty years.

One day, the boss, Mr. Pollard, showed up to visit with his old friend Mr. Gandy. He sympathized with my injury and asked me how the summer had been. I told him that I had never worked so hard in my life and had never seen a worse place to be in the summer. He smiled and told me I could go to work for his company after I graduated from college if I wanted to.

The rest of the crew finished cutting across Carvers Bay and reached the Great Pee Dee River soon after Labor Day. On October 15, 1954, Hurricane Hazel hit near Georgetown and badly damaged the coast of South Carolina. A year later, a contract was let to build the canal along the centerline that we had established. The canal was eventually completed and continues to bring fresh water to the mill and to the city of Georgetown.

Bibliography

Alston, J. Motte. *Rice Planter and Sportsman: The Recollections of J. Motte Alston, 1821–1909*. Edited by Arney R. Childs. Columbia: University of South Carolina Press, 1999.

Babcock, Blakely B. *Jonathan Buck of Bucksport*. Ellsworth, ME: Ellsworth American, 1975.

Bishop, Nathaniel H. *Voyage of the Paper Canoe*. Boston: Lee and Shephard, 1878.

Bridwell, Ronald E. *Gem of the Atlantic Seaboard*. Georgetown, SC: Georgetown Times, 1991.

Buck, Alice F. *Bucksport, Past and Present*. Bucksport, ME: 1951.

Burroughs, Franklin. *Horry and the Waccamaw*. New York: W.W. Norton & Co., 1992.

Cely, John. *Cowasee Basin*. Manning, SC: Totally Outdoors Publishing Inc., 2011.

Chapelle, Howard I. *The History of American Sailing Ships*. New York: W.W. Norton, 1935.

Dusinberre, William. *Them Dark Days*. Athens: University of Georgia Press, 1996.

Earley, Lawrence S. *Looking for Longleaf: The Rise and Fall of an American Forest.* Chapel Hill: University of North Carolina Press, 2004.

Edgar, Walter. *South Carolina: A History.* Columbia: University of South Carolina Press, 1998.

Estep, H. Cole. *How Wooden Ships Are Built.* New York: W.W. Norton, 1918.

Gilmore, James R. *Among the Pines.* New York: J.R. Gilmore, 1862.

Independent Republic Quarterly. Horry County Historical Society, Conway, SC. Various articles authored by Charles Joyner, Eugenia Buck Cutts, Constance Fournier, Sharyn B. Holliday, Charles Dusenbury and William H. Pendleton.

Joyner, Charles. *Down by the Riverside.* Chicago: University of Illinois Press, 1984.

Matthews, Frederick C. *American Merchant Ships, 1850–1900.* New York: Dover Publications, 1987.

Owens, Mary E. *Bucksport, South Carolina.* Self-published, 2008.

Phillips, Ulrich Bonnell. *A History of Transportation in the Eastern Cotton Belt to 1860.* New York: Columbia University Press, 1908.

Pilkey, Orrin H., and Mary Edna Fraser. *A Celebration of the World's Barrier Islands.* New York: Columbia University Press, 2003.

Rogers, George C., Jr. *The History of Georgetown County, South Carolina.* Columbia: University of South Carolina Press, 1970.

Waterhouse, Richard. *A New World Gentry: The Making of a Merchant and Planter Class in South Carolina, 1670–1770.* Charleston, SC: The History Press, 2005.

Wood, Virginia Steele. *Live Oaking.* Annapolis, MD: Naval Institute Press, 1981.

Woodward, C. Vann, and Elisabeth Muhlenfeld. *The Private Mary Chesnut.* New York: Oxford University Press, 1984.

Index

A

ACE Basin 87, 89
Allston, Robert F.W. 34
Alston, J. Motte 30, 32

B

Bath, ME 25, 41, 56, 69
Beidler, Francis 90
Bishop, Nathaniel 39
Black River 34, 94, 98, 101
Buck, Desiah McGilvery 33, 35, 39, 42, 56
Buck, Henry L. 36
Buck, Jonathan 16
Buck, Richard Pike 26, 31
Bucksport, ME 13, 16, 23, 25, 26, 28, 31, 37, 39, 64
Bucksport, SC 9, 27, 33, 36, 39, 59, 64
Bucksville, ME 9
Bucksville, SC 9, 27, 28, 38, 43, 44, 48, 61, 64
Buck, William L. 37, 42, 59, 61

C

Cape Hatteras 25, 38

Cape Romain 90
Carvers Bay 89, 103, 105, 106
Chesnut, Mary Boykin 34
Civilian Conservation Corps 86
Clark, Mary 23, 26
Clyde Steamship Line 58, 62, 65, 66
Congaree National Park 8, 11, 91
Conwayborough 16, 17, 26, 27, 28, 40, 59

D

Downeaster 41, 42, 69
Dunbar, Elisha 39, 42, 44, 50
DuPont 74
Dusenbury, Charles 9, 46, 47, 48
Dusenbury, James 38
Dusenbury, Z.W. 40

F

Flint, Charles Ranlett 69, 72
Forest Legacy Program 89
Francis Marion National Forest 86, 93

G

Georgetown & Western Railroad 73
Gilbert, Cephas 33, 36

Gilmore, James 27, 33
Grissetts Landing 17

H

Hampton, Harry 7, 90, 91
Hampton, Wade 59, 61
Hebron 9, 28, 37, 46
Horry, Peter 17
Hot and Hot Fish Club 14

K

Kaminski, Heiman 55, 58
Kobe, Japan 54, 55

L

Lafayette, Marquis Gilbert 97
live oak 16, 22, 90

M

Marion, Francis 17
McGilvery, William 28, 29, 31, 33, 35,
        37, 38, 39, 41, 42, 48, 51, 56
Myrtle Beach 64, 94

N

National Recovery Act 86
Nature Conservancy 87, 88, 89, 90
naval stores 19, 25, 28, 36, 40, 56, 64,
        65, 66, 67, 95
Nickels, Jonathan C. 41
Norman, Frances 27
Norman, Sarah Jane 17

P

Pee Dee 95
Pee Dee River 14, 36, 40, 65, 67, 88,
        89, 93, 98, 106
Penobscot River 16, 25, 39

R

Ross, A.M. 51

S

Sampit River 17, 72, 94
Sandy Island 88
Santee River 67, 86, 87, 89, 94
Searsport, ME 9, 16, 23, 25, 26, 28,
        31, 33, 35, 38, 39, 41, 42, 43,
        50, 51, 52, 53, 55, 56
South Carolina Department of Natural
        Resources 83, 87
South Carolina Forestry Commission
        9, 81, 85
South Carolina Public Service
        Authority 86

T

Tip Top 33, 40, 88

U

Upper Mill 9, 26, 27, 37, 64

W

Waccamaw (brig) 32, 35
Waccamaw Neck 32, 89
Waccamaw River 11, 14, 16, 17, 24,
        26, 27, 28, 29, 32, 36, 38, 40,
        46, 65, 67, 74, 88, 89, 93
Winyah Bay 14, 16, 25, 32, 38, 47, 67,
        72, 82, 87, 89, 93, 94, 95, 97, 98
Woodbourne 30, 32
Woodbury 89
Woodbury, Stephen E. 56

About the Author

Robert McAlister is a retired construction manager. He and his wife, Mary, have lived in or near Georgetown, South Carolina, for much of the past sixty years. They are participants in the activities of the South Carolina Maritime Museum in Georgetown. He has written *The Life and Times of Georgetown Sea Captain Abram Jones Slocum, 1861–1914* and *Wooden Ships on Winyah Bay*, both published by The History Press. He has also written *Cruising Through Life*, a memoir of his family's sailing adventures.

Visit us at
www.historypress.net
....
This title is also available as an e-book